The Parent's Book about Bullying

Changing the Course of Your Child's Life

William Voors

With a Foreword by Dorothy L. Espelage, Ph.D.

■ HAZELDEN®

INFORMATION & EDUCATIONAL SERVICES

Hazelden
Center City, Minnesota 55012-0176

1-800-328-0094
1-651-213-4590 (Fax)
www.hazelden.org

Library of Congress Cataloging-in-Publication Data
Voors, William, 1950–
   The parent's book about bullying : changing the course of your child's
life : for parents on either side of the bullying fence / William Voors ;
with a foreword by Dorothy L. Espelage.
      p. cm.
Includes bibliographical references (p.) and index.
ISBN 1-56838-517-X (paperback)
1. Bullying. 2. Child rearing. I. Title.

BF637.B85 V66 2000
649'.64—dc21   00-040916

04 03 02   6 5 4 3

Cover design by David Spohn
Interior design and typesetting by Spaulding & Kinne

Voors, William

Bullying : changing the course of your child's life

The Parent's Book about Bullying

Contents

Foreword

For several decades, researchers in many nations have documented the serious consequences associated with bullying, and some countries have implemented national campaigns to protect children from peer harassment. Unfortunately, U.S. scholars are only now beginning to recognize bullying as a serious concern for youth. We are therefore a long way from a complete understanding of this aggressive behavior and even further from instituting large-scale prevention and intervention programs in schools. Given that almost every adult can remember being bullied, bullying someone else, or witnessing these events during their childhoods, the delay in officially recognizing the destructiveness of peer harassment among U.S. children and adolescents is somewhat surprising. While researchers have much more to learn about bullying, parents need a resource *now* to inform them about what *is* known.

William Voors provides just that in *The Parent's Book about Bullying*. His comprehensive understanding of the research literature on bullying is apparent. He clearly defines the broad range of bullying behaviors and discusses how societal attitudes among adults model and encourage peer harassment. He provides lists of behavioral and psychological signs to help parents assess if their child may be a target or instigator of bullying. The book also guides parents through initiating conversation about bullying with their children and putting into practice practical suggestions to help their children overcome self-defeating behaviors.

In his advice to parents, William Voors also draws from many years of clinical experience counseling children and adolescents who have been bullied, bullied others, or witnessed bullying. As a result, the book is filled with engaging illustrative case examples. Although this book is written specifically for parents, all adults will find the information useful. As Mr. Voors states in the epilogue: "Fighting the battle against peer abuse requires a concerted effort on the part of parents, schools, the legal system, and the community at large."

Dorothy L. Espelage, Ph.D.
Assistant Professor
Department of Educational Psychology
University of Illinois at Urbana-Champaign

Acknowledgments

I would like to thank everyone who played a part in helping me complete this book. First, I want to thank Cynthia Harris, my editor at Hazelden, who has been a fount of patience and wisdom. I also want to thank my agent, Jane Jordan Browne, and Janie McAdams, who provided editorial assistance. There are many other people—family, friends, and colleagues—who helped by reading, critiquing, providing professional advice, or just being there for me during this process. There are far too many to list, but you know who you are, and your support is appreciated more than you know. I want to thank my parents, who gave me life and taught me how to live; my sons, for the gift of themselves and the joy and privilege of being their father; and most especially my wife, who blesses my life in countless ways.

Introduction

Imagine you're standing in line at the grocery store after a long day at work. You're tired, you're hungry, and your mind wanders. As you lean on your shopping cart patiently waiting, you reflect upon the day's events. A smile bubbles up as you recall a funny incident as your child left for school that morning. You feel thankful that you're the parent of such a terrific young person. Suddenly, the solid smack of a hand against the side of your head interrupts your pleasant reverie. Your ear rings with the impact, and as you bring up your hand to protect yourself, you hear someone say, "Hey, I'm in a hurry, let me in front of you." You turn to see a customer jamming his cart in front of yours, forcing your cart backward and almost knocking you over. You can tell by the customer's attitude that you had better let him have his way or you may be seriously hurt. He's smiling and appears to be enjoying himself. You look around to see if other shoppers will come to your aid, but they walk by as if you were invisible, and no one seems to notice. In a public place where you expect to be safe, your safety is seriously jeopardized.

An avalanche of feelings—anger, shock, humiliation, helplessness, and fear—overcomes you as you try to decide what to do next. You need to react in some way. Will you contact the manager? Ignore the perpetrator? Demand your place in line back? Call the police?

You may say this scenario is absurd. Admittedly, it's an unlikely one for adults. We don't expect adults to behave this way toward other adults, and we don't tolerate this kind of behavior. However, children are expected to put up with similar situations every day in their neighborhoods and, especially, at school. In environments where they should be safe from harm, children are subjected to every manner of abuse from other children—from name-calling to exclusion to physical assault. To make matters worse, the abuse is often ignored or minimized by many adults simply because the instigators are children. It's as if we believe that children can't hurt one another to the degree that adults can hurt other adults or children.

Bullying is a term that applies to the behavior of anyone who mistreats another human being by using physical strength, authority, or social or intellectual leverage. Not only a label for children, the term *bully* applies just as easily to adults who abuse children or other adults, including spouses or partners. But labels, such as "bully" or "victim," identify the behavior with the individual and are counterproductive. Labeling language can trap the children we want to help. When we label children, we reinforce our perception that the behavior they're exhibiting in the bullying situation is permanent. Therefore, I refer to the instigators of bullying as *children who bully,* and to the children they bully as *targets.* Although both terms may at first feel awkward, they remove any idea of blame from either party and allow parents to work with their children in more understanding ways.

A more accurate clinical term for bullying between children is *peer abuse,* but it has not yet reached common usage. In fact most of us have never heard the term. Yet many human interactions now deemed unacceptable in our society plagued our culture for decades, or even centuries, before identification changed the public's awareness. A new term often allows us to see behavior in a new light. Child abuse, violence against children by adults, is a good example. It has only been in the last generation that we as a culture have recognized that the mistreatment of children is a serious social problem. Prior to the 1970s, child abuse was rarely reported and often ignored. In 1974 Congress passed the Child Abuse Prevention and Treatment Act, finally providing children with some measure of protection from physical and emotional abuse.

As parents we want our children to be safe. We want them

to like school, to participate in activities that interest them, to discover who they are, and to enjoy their friends. In short, we want them to have happy childhoods. But in schools where I conduct seminars, students routinely report that bullying is a "big problem." Whether the school is inner-city or suburban, public or private, the response is the same. Peer abuse is a serious and pervasive concern for students.

A number of studies point to the tremendous impact peer abuse has on children. In a study of rural midwestern children published in 1993, 90 percent of fourth- through eighth-graders said they had been the target of bullying at some point during their school careers.[1] The results of a widely respected study published around the same time reveal that 20 percent of children who report having been bullied say it caused them serious social and emotional problems.[2] The most recent data collected by the National Education Association and the U.S. Department of Justice estimates that 160,000 children miss school each day to avoid attacks or threats made by fellow students.[3] But children who bully also suffer. Not only do some of these children have greater problems with impulsivity and inappropriate expression of anger, they also tend to be more depressed and are more likely to feel as though they don't belong at school than children who don't bully.

Most research has focused on the emotional toll that peer abuse takes during childhood. The results of the small amount of research that has explored the long-term impact of chronic peer abuse on career and economic success are alarming. Both targets and instigators have lower academic performance and higher dropout rates, leading to diminished expectations and severely limited potentials over the course of their lifetimes.

Targets of bullying can even tend toward extreme violence, not only to themselves but toward others. It's impossible to deny the destructiveness of bullying when we look at a few of the tragedies spawned by chronic abuse. One beautiful Florida morning a few years ago, a twelve-year-old boy was found hanging from a tree in his backyard. He had committed suicide when the pain of being taunted by his classmates had become too much to bear. In Georgia, a boy who had been mercilessly harassed about his weight walked to the front of his middle school classroom, said he couldn't take the abuse anymore, pulled a gun from his book bag, and killed himself. The emotional assaults these boys had suffered had eaten away at their hearts.

The 1998–99 school year rendered a horrific trail of carnage in middle schools and high schools across the United States. A common thread among most of the perpetrators was that they had been targets of chronic peer abuse. Fortunately, targets of bullying seldom instigate such disasters; however, these tragedies convey the desperation and horrendous pain that children who experience bullying can feel.

Despite the rash of extreme school violence in the past several years, schools remain a relatively safe place for children to be. Extreme physical violence, the likes of which we saw in Littleton, Colorado; Paducah, Kentucky; Jonesboro, Arkansas; and Pearl, Mississippi, is rare. Although very few children will become victims or witnesses of such tragedy, our children are not as safe as they should be.

Some parents of children who instigate bullying spend much of their time worrying that their children are not learning to get along with others. These parents live with the constant fear that the school will call to report another problem. They are perplexed about why their child behaves inappropriately and frustrated that their numerous attempts to change the aggressive behavior have proved unfruitful. When envisioning their child's future, they may see an adult life marked with violence and dysfunctional relationships because of entrenched behaviors and attitudes. Other parents of children who bully may be unaware of the seriousness of their child's behavior and sometimes may feel a need to defend their child's actions.

Parents whose children are targets of bullying worry that their children will suffer through cycles of abuse at the hands of their peers. They may fear that their children will be crippled by low self-esteem and an inability to form close relationships in adulthood.

As parents who have high hopes for our children, it can be difficult to acknowledge that our own behavior may contribute to our child's difficulties. Parents of any child who instigates bullying may unwittingly model bullying behavior when they use inappropriate behavior to deal with problems. Some parents—especially overprotective ones—take ineffective roles in defending their children from bullying, further exacerbating their child's role as a target.

Part of my motivation for writing this book is that as a child I endured verbal peer abuse. In addition to this painful role as target, I was also a bystander to the abuse of schoolmates. I remember the helplessness and anger I felt at seeing another kid get picked on. So it pains me to hear accounts of children who are bullied. But my heart also goes out to those children who instigate bullying; I understand they do so because they are undergoing emotional confusion, not because they are "bad" kids. I am dismayed because I know the untold damage that childhood peer abuse inflicts not only on children, but also on the adults those children become. I've talked with many adults who suffer from depression, anxiety, social phobias, and relationship problems that we can trace back to the peer abuse they experienced as children. When I ask my adult clients whether they were ever bullied as children and if the bullying has affected their lives, a surprising number respond with a resounding "yes," as if they've been waiting for someone to ask the question. Each time I hear a client recall painful memories of being a target of peer abuse, I'm struck by the pervasive influence of bullying across the life span. I've also counseled many adults who as children instigated bullying. Many of these people have continued to depend on this destructive behavior as adults, resulting in dysfunctional relationships, broken families, and sometimes criminal behavior.

Few adults understand that the abuse of children by other children presents a serious threat to the mental health of today's youth and tomorrow's adults. Prevention of peer abuse and treatment—for targets as well as instigators of bullying—is the next frontier of mental health. Why do we still so easily accept the myth that a certain amount of violence against a child is normal if committed by a child, yet wrong if committed by an adult? Just as we did in the 1970s with the issue of child abuse, we must now face the reality that peer abuse is a correctable social ill.

We need to change the cultural norms that allow bullying to continue, and parents are in a pivotal role to make this happen. As long as we keep buying into erroneous and dangerous notions such as "Kids will be kids," "Sticks and stones will break your bones but words will never hurt you," and "Might makes right," we can expect an even more violent school culture. Violence isn't easily tamed. We know that metal detectors, stricter gun laws, school crisis plans, armed guards, and tougher laws to crack down on violent offenders won't solve the problem. What will help to solve the problem is a societal change of attitude and behaviors.

But societal change is a slow process. The fact that you're reading this book means that you're probably looking for answers to address pressing concerns about your child. Both instigators and targets of bullying need to learn how to fully accept themselves and others as they are. They need to learn how to get their own needs met while working cooperatively with others. This book will help you teach your child the skills to feel more confident, to be assertive when necessary, to handle anger and frustration more appropriately, and to get along with others more peaceably.

As parents, we are our children's most important teachers. It's essential that we actively teach compassion, empathy, assertiveness, and self-respect to our children by modeling it ourselves. When we help our children modify their behavior, we're taking a giant step toward helping the next generation live happier, more productive lives. The lessons we teach our children will differ depending on whether they are targets of bullying or children who bully, but we can all help our children understand themselves and one another.

Section 1

THE PROBLEM OF BULLYING

1

What Bullying Is

According to Ecclesiastes, there's nothing new under the sun. The same types of bullying are going on now that went on some forty years ago when I was a child. However, the bullying we now see has become more intense, more highly sexualized at earlier ages, and more potentially damaging due to an overall societal coarsening and a desensitization to violence.

Not all conflict can be classified as bullying. Children will always fight and argue among themselves. Normal confrontational behavior crosses the line and becomes bullying when certain criteria are met. One of the two scenarios below constitutes bullying and the other does not.

Scenario 1

Sam is a fourth-grader who wants to play kickball, but Kevin says he can't because he's too slow. Sam, who has never had a problem with Kevin before, says it doesn't matter if he's slow, he wants to play anyway. Sam grabs the kickball from Kevin and says he's going to play. Kevin pushes Sam, knocking him down, and they start to fight.

Scenario 2

Alex, another fourth-grader, also wants to play kickball. He is one of the largest boys in the class, but he is awkward and clumsy at sports. He tells Geoffrey that he wants to play and Geoffrey says sure, but Kevin yells that Alex can't play because "he's a sissy and he kicks like a girl." Then Kevin starts to laugh, and several other boys laugh along with him. Geoffrey doesn't laugh, but he doesn't stand up for Alex either. Alex says, "All right," and goes to sit by himself away from the kickball game. He feels embarrassed and frustrated because this is the third day in a row Kevin has called him a sissy and humiliated him on the playground.

■ ■ ■

The first situation involved a poorly handled conflict between the two boys, but it was not bullying. Fighting is not unusual for boys of this age. Some boys will tussle from time to time as they gradually learn to deal with their differences in socially acceptable ways. These boys were relative equals, and Ben was not afraid of Kevin. Ben, who asserted himself clearly with Kevin, wasn't about to be put off just because Kevin didn't want him to play.

The second scenario fits our definition of bullying: *Bullying occurs whenever one or more persons enjoy using power to repeatedly and consistently harm one or more people.* We can break down this definition into three criteria.

1. There must be *repeated and consistent negative actions* against the child. Children are naturally resilient and can usually deal with isolated, unrelated incidents of meanness, as Ben did in the first scenario. But bullying means that

abuse happens regularly and for the same reasons, resulting in the constant wearing down of the child's self-esteem. This was the third time in a week that Kevin had harassed Alex for the same reason. As happens with targets of bullying, every time the abuse occurred Alex felt a little more humiliated than the previous time.

2. There must be an *imbalance of power* between the child who bullies and the target. The child who bullies is stronger physically, verbally, or socially, leaving the target feeling overwhelmed and unable to deal with the abuse. It's important to realize that the imbalance need not be size. Sometimes a smaller child can humiliate and demean a larger child because the target doesn't possess the verbal skills to respond with confidence. Though Alex was larger than most of the boys in his class, he was easily put down by Kevin, who hit a nerve when he called Alex a sissy, and Alex did not know what to say. Having few or less popular children for friends and low self-confidence can also lead to an imbalance of social power between two children.

3. There must be *contrasting feelings* between the child who bullies and the target as a result of the bullying episode. The child who bullies may feel excited, powerful, or amused after the bullying incident while the target feels afraid, embarrassed, or hurt. There were no contrasting feelings between Ben and Kevin. They were both angry. However, while Kevin was laughing and enjoying himself, Alex felt sheepish and afraid, causing him to retire in humiliation to the other side of the playground. Targets often feel hurt and angry when children who bully attack them. If they try to express the hurt or anger, the bullying child usually responds with indifference or mockery, which leads to even more humiliation.

Bullying encompasses a broad range of behaviors that fall into three broad categories: physical, verbal, and relational bullying.

Physical Bullying

Examples of physical bullying almost always come up first when I ask elementary-age through middle-school-age children to provide a definition of bullying. Common forms of physical bullying in the early elementary grades include kicking, pushing, shoving, hitting, spitting, pulling hair, biting, and locking a child in an enclosed space. As children reach the later elementary, middle school, and high school years, physical bullying can become more violent, as well as more sexually oriented. Humiliating acts, such as swirlies (holding someone's head in a flushing toilet), wedgies (pulling up someone's underwear), and depantsing, become more common. Unwanted sexual touching is a common problem for girls, especially those who are developing more rapidly than their peers and whom boys consider attractive. As boys develop physically, muscle mass and strength increase, and consequently physical bullying becomes more intense. Bullying becomes more dangerous when older children attach hateful ideologies to their bullying, as in gay-bashing and supremacist groups. Children who bully will sometimes resort to firearms and other weapons, which have become a prominent threat in schools across this country.

Physical bullying is the easiest type of peer abuse to identify. It's easy to see when someone is being assaulted. It's also the one type of bullying that most people can agree *is* bullying. Although many in our society trivialize emotional abuse, most people recognize that physical abuse is unacceptable.

Verbal Bullying

Whoever said "Sticks and stones will break your bones, but words will never hurt you" was probably never bullied verbally. It's a lie to tell children that words can't hurt them. None of us appreciates hearing hurtful things. Verbal threats, swearing, name-calling, and cruel jokes about clothes and other possessions, appearance, disabilities, race, ethnic background, religion, or idiosyncrasies are all forms of verbal bullying. Children are even more sensitive than adults to verbal abuse since they have not yet developed a firm sense of who they are. Peers' comments play a critical role in establishing that sense of self, according to developmental psychologist Lesa Rae Vartanian, who states that "other's words are grist for the identity mill."[1] Children listen to their peers, and what they hear matters to them. Children are works in progress, and the words of peers serve to tell them not only who others think they are, but who they should be and who they will be. A girl who is consistently told she's fat and ugly in eighth grade may not only stay away from tryouts for high school plays, though acting in one has been a long-time dream, but she may also become anorexic in an attempt to prove her detractors wrong. A boy who is told he's a wuss in fifth grade may not only avoid trying out for basketball, he may experiment with drugs in middle school as a way to fit in somewhere since he can't identify with the jocks.

Verbal bullying is the most common form of bullying among boys and girls from grade school through high school. One difference between a third-grader and a tenth-grader is the level of sophistication of their speech. While the third-grader may call someone "dumbie," a high school student may ironically say, "Oh, look. Here comes Roberto. He's 'mentally challenged,' you know."

The abuse tends to get worse as children get older, and by middle school it can be brutal. When I ask middle school students what bothers them most about going to school, the answers are fairly predictable:

- "Kids are so mean. If you're a girl at our school, you're either a whore if you have a boyfriend, or you're a lezzie if you don't."
- "I hate going to PE because I get called fat-ass every day."
- "School is awful for some kids. I cry sometimes when I think about a friend of mine who's called names just because her face breaks out. It's not her fault."

Verbal bullying is easier to get away with than is physical bullying. Of all types of bullying, verbal peer abuse takes the least amount of time and can be very subtle. Sometimes it happens unnoticed right under the noses of teachers and other adults. Some people call verbal bullying teasing. But "teasing" is appropriate only when applied to a playful situation, when all parties are having fun and hurting another's feelings isn't the intent. When a child is verbally abused, it's important to classify the abuse as bullying, because this term conveys the seriousness of the behavior to the instigator and bystanders and validates the child who has been targeted.

Verbal bullying isn't benign, cute, funny, or clever. Verbal bullying is a powerful and damaging form of emotional abuse that can negatively affect a person throughout a lifetime.

Relational Bullying

Human beings have probably always ostracized, or excluded, those who don't seem to fit in. Formal shunning, such as we see in religious groups or labor organizations, is usually perceived by the participants as having a useful social purpose—to unify the group and to reinforce the values held by the group. The word *ostracize* comes from the ancient Greek *ostraca*, a type of pottery that documented formal votes on who should be banished from the community. Some religious groups, such as the Old Order Amish, practice formal shunning when a member of the community breaks an inviolable rule. After that point, no one in the community, even a family member, is allowed to talk to or recognize the shunned person in any way. It's as if that person doesn't exist. Our prison system is a form of exclusion. We separate those who break inviolable rules so they don't have contact with mainstream society. Although it's not always fair and far from an ideal solution, formal shunning makes it clear that certain antisocial behaviors that severely disrupt a society's equilibrium will not be tolerated.

Unlike formal shunning that's condoned by a society as a way to reduce antisocial behavior and therefore enhance the quality of life, shunning among young people is arbitrarily cruel. A young person may be shunned because of the way he or she looks, acts, or thinks. This kind of shunning doesn't prevent antisocial behavior—it *is* antisocial behavior. It is a form of relational bullying. Shunning makes clear who belongs within the culture and who doesn't, and punishes those who don't fit the membership criteria by treating them as if they don't matter. This type of peer abuse tends to be most common among girls entering puberty. Sometimes relational bullying can start with a minor fracas or disagreement between two students, and bystanders will jump on board to play "Let's be mean to Sara today." Others may not make eye contact with a child who is shunned or may not respond when the shunned child speaks to them. When shunning happens in the school setting, especially as children enter adolescence, the damage to a child's self-esteem can be particularly harmful. At this age, when adolescents are beginning to break away from the family and form identities within their social group, they need to feel free to explore who they are without being judged. To be actively rejected and isolated at a time when peer acceptance is most important can be excruciating. The result may be various psychiatric problems, including depression and a reliance upon alcohol and other drugs to escape a sense of alienation.

Gossip, another form of relational bullying, may take the form of spreading malicious lies or rumors or writing nasty notes about someone in a public place, such as a restroom, locker room, or bulletin board. At first glance, gossip may seem to fall into the category of verbal bullying, but it differs from verbal bullying in an important way. In verbal bullying, the harmful words are aimed directly at the target. In gossip, the aim is indirect, but the result is just as harmful. The target of gossip feels the effects of alienation and rejection but may not know why because he hasn't even heard the insults.

Relational bullying thrives in a climate that separates and classifies young people into cliques. Cliques have always been part of the middle school and high school culture. Cliques give young people the opportunity to belong, to feel accepted, and to be a part of a special group. Populars, jocks, brains, normals, loners, and druggies are cliques that typically become well defined by high school. Other schools may also have cliques like gang-bangers (gang member wanna-bes), Goths (who share a fascination with nihilism, anarchy, and sometimes Satanism), surfer cliques, ethnic cliques, or supremacist cliques. A particularly menacing form of clique is the criminal youth gang. Gangs were once primarily an urban problem, but in recent years suburban and rural gangs have become more widespread.

Some cliques appear to promote positive values such as athletics or academics, while some cliques clearly do not. The real problem with cliques is that in order to belong, a child must think or behave in a certain way. Kids who are considered outcasts or who do not belong to popular cliques are often subjected to cruel and persistent relational bullying and run the risk of turning to a clique that promotes unhealthy or dangerous behavior. Especially at the high school level, tensions can rise high between cliques on the opposite ends of the social ladder—for example, between the jocks and the Goths.

Bullying and Humor

In its most insidious form, bullying involves a cruel form of humor. When children associate humor with violence in a bullying situation, they are likely to become desensitized to another person's pain. Just as a person cannot feel anger and emotional warmth at the same time, one cannot experience cruel humor and empathy for another person at the same time. If a child finds a bullying situation humorous—for example, laughing when someone calls a schoolmate "Fatso" or when a girl's head is dunked in a swirling toilet—it's as if the child is watching a movie for his or her entertainment rather than watching a living, feeling human being in pain. The desensitization that causes bystanders to become less and less affected by peer abuse makes the abuse more likely to happen again. Their laughter reinforces the instigator's perception that nothing is wrong with the behavior. Of course, the target suffers tremendously as well. When others stand around and laugh, the child's suffering becomes a joke, and he or she loses confidence in the compassion of others. The target soon feels as if nobody cares about his or her plight.

Bullying behavior troubles most adults, yet peer abuse—among both children and adults—is tolerated by far too many of us. When any form of abuse is tolerated, it will persist. We should not be surprised that peer abuse occurs so often wherever children gather. Bullying is a problem among children because it's a problem in our society at large. To reduce or eliminate peer abuse, we must address the underlying causes that provide the societal foundation that supports antisocial behavior. We must understand how we adults can help stop the cycle of abuse.

2

Societal Attitudes toward Bullying

Every child and adult deserves to be treated with respect. Yet every day our children absorb societal attitudes that not only minimize and deny but also sometimes embrace intolerance. To discover where kids learn to be cruel to one another, we need look no further than newspaper headlines, movies, or television. Ours is a violent society.

One-third of all injury deaths in the United States are due to intentional injury.[1] In 1997, firearms were the third leading cause of death for children ages ten to fourteen, and the second leading cause of death for ages fifteen to twenty-four.[2] The same year, the number of deaths by firearms among children fourteen or younger in the United States was nearly twelve times higher than the combined rate in twenty-five other industrialized nations.[3]

Despite these startlingly high numbers of violent deaths, most adults abhor the violence that is woven through the fabric of society, but they have become desensitized. It takes so much to shock us now that many of us take notice of only the most extreme violence, like school shootings or acts of torture that stem from racial or sexual intolerance. Our attention span lasts only a few short weeks until the media frenzy dies.

We've learned to tune out much violence, but tuning it out doesn't make it go away, and it will get worse until we address the underlying causes. A major cause, if not *the* major cause, is our minimization of bullying. As long as disrespect is something to be snickered at or ignored and bullying behavior continues to be tolerated, we will find it impossible to create kinder, more compassionate communities in our schools and neighborhoods. And the lack of kind and compassionate communities will lead, in turn, to more instances of peer abuse among children who fail to understand the severe consequences of their violent behavior.

The Minimization of Bullying

The most common form of violence children experience is bullying, and much of it takes place at school. The most effective deterrent to bullying is adult intervention. Yet too many adults, including some educators, believe bullying is an insignificant issue. We don't advocate often enough for children who are bullied, though we'd probably advocate for an adult who complained of the same behavior from a co-worker or a partner. Most adults want to see an end to bullying, but even caring adults often minimize complaints about bullying as overreactions. Sometimes they poke fun at targets of bullying for making a fuss or for not standing up for themselves. When asked how often teachers intervene in bullying situations, students in a study responded that teachers intervene 25 percent of the time. When asked the same question, 71 percent of the teachers said they always intervene.[4] Tragically, many students believe neither their parents nor adults at school would listen or care if they had a problem with bullying.[5] Misconceptions abound regarding what bullying is and what to do about it. To recognize how serious a problem bullying really is, we need to dispel these myths.

Myths about Bullying

Myth 1: All Bullying Is Physical

When I ask youngsters to define bullying, their first responses are almost always the same: fighting, hitting, kicking, and shoving. Like most adults, these children mistakenly believe that all bullying involves physical confrontations, when, in fact, verbal peer abuse is much more prevalent than physical abuse. The most common form of bullying is name-calling. And when children reach the upper elementary and middle school grades, relational bullying becomes more frequent, especially among girls. Few people recognize verbal or relational bullying as abuse. This, I believe, is because our society condones emotional abuse. Popular talk show hosts build reputations on their ability to deliver crude put-downs, and movies and television shows capitalize on insulting jokes to get laughs. Recognizing all types of bullying as abuse eliminates the ambiguity that allows our children to suffer.

Myth 2: Bullying Is Just Playing Around

Toby was an overweight fifth-grader who since third grade had been the target of a small group of boys. One day when the physical education teacher left the gym for a moment, he returned to find Toby stranded twenty feet in the air at the top of the climbing rope and the same three boys taunting him to come down. "Hey, Lardass, get your fat butt down here." A small group of bystanders watched and laughed, though most of the class stood back and pretended to ignore the situation. Toby had climbed the rope to escape threats of being depantsed and sent out into the hall. When the principal asked the three perpetrators to explain their behavior, one of them said they were just playing around and didn't mean anything by it.

We should not allow anyone to get away with the worn-out excuses "I was just kidding" or "We were just having some fun." Certainly, play is necessary for children to learn social skills. Cooperation, sharing, mutual respect, and reciprocity are learned through play and games, and playful teasing can be a way for friends or siblings to show their affection—a way to say, "When I'm with you, I can relax and I don't have to take myself that seriously." But hurting someone else, whether physically or emotionally, is never funny and should always be taken seriously.

Myth 3: Bullying Is Normal Peer Conflict

After Jennifer—a popular fourth-grader—called a new student a "nigger" and spit on her, the school counselor called Jennifer's mother to come to her office. Jennifer's racist language and behavior violated the school's zero-tolerance policy for bullying. When confronted with this information, Jennifer's mother smiled sweetly and said, "I've talked with Jennifer about this many times. I don't know what gets into her. But you know," she continued with an exasperated sigh, "you can't stop this stuff. . . . Kids will be kids."

Conflict and even aggression are inevitable aspects of any meaningful social relationship among children, and learning how to resolve conflict is a social skill children must learn as they mature. Learning give-and-take is not easy. The normal egocentrism that accompanies youth gets in the way of respectful problem solving. It's natural for very young children to have a Ptolemaic view of the world. Just as humans once believed the sun revolved around the earth, young children believe that everything revolves around them. On the way to learning the value of cooperation, empathy, and compromise, conflict will occur. In the early grades (K–2), children don't always think of others. Their play and their choice of friends is based on getting what they want. When this need is frustrated, a common response is to reject another child.

Given a healthy, stable home and school environment, a

child grows out of this youthful self-centeredness and becomes aware of and learns to value the needs of others. We're all interrelated, and the more children become aware of these connections, the more socialized they become. Games with rules become more important, and the idea of compromise begins to develop. Fairness becomes a major bone of contention, and conflict occurs when rules are broken.

But the child who bullies has no interest in mutual give-and-take. This child singles out and torments someone who is weaker either physically, intellectually, or socially and develops a sense of superiority and entitlement. Unlike the youngster who may reject a peer out of selfishness, the child who bullies rejects the other child because she believes she is *better than* the other person and therefore has the *right* to bully.

Since children who bully have not developed normal socialization skills, the saying "Kids will be kids" is not appropriate when applied to their abusive behavior. This dangerous rationalization of their cruelty enables bullying to continue under a cloak of normalcy. Normalizing abusive behavior is practically a guarantee that it will continue. We must hold children accountable for their bullying behavior, even at an early age, so they learn that it's unacceptable.

Myth 4: Bullying Is Only a Boy's Issue

When many adults conjure an image of a child who bullies, they picture a boy. Boys tend to be more physical than girls, often making them more visible in the school and in the neighborhood. Boys are also more likely to admit to bullying and are even proud of the fact, especially in elementary and middle school. But girls bully as well, and they can be every bit as cruel as boys can be. Although girls are involved to a lesser extent in physical peer abuse than boys are, they are just as likely as boys to bully verbally, and more likely than boys to use relational bullying, such as gossip and exclusion.

Cross-gender bullying happens, too. Boys can bully girls,

and vice versa. Most cross-gender bullying is sexual harassment, even at young ages. Sexual harassment is any unwanted verbal, nonverbal, or physical behavior of a sexual nature. Here are some examples:

- A first-grade girl laughs at another first-grader because he is a boy but he throws "like a girl."
- A fourth-grade boy calls a female classmate a "ho."
- A seventh-grade girl is standing with a group of girl-friends talking about their favorite boys. A male classmate walks by and one of the girls points at him laughing, and says, "What about him?" Another girl says, "No way!" and all the girls laugh.
- A fifth-grade girl is humiliated by a couple of boys in class who leer at her and often tell her they'd like to have sex with her.

Myth 5: Bullying or Being Bullied Has No Lasting Effects

Peer abuse has been normalized to such an extent that most adults really believe it doesn't affect the developing personalities of children in any serious or long-lasting way. We often view peer abuse as a phase that children just grow out of as they mature.

Kids outgrow some behaviors and attitudes on their own, but the dysfunctional pattern of bullying isn't one of them. Bullying behaviors tend to have lifelong consequences if not corrected in the early years. Antisocial adults were usually antisocial children. As a society, it's dangerous for us to think of bullying as a stage kids outgrow. Our prisons are filled with adults who were once children who bullied.

Although children do not outgrow bullying on their own, they can be *helped* to overcome bullying problems. Bullying is a learned behavior. That's good news because any behavior that is learned can be changed. But unless abusive patterns are recognized, the child who instigates bullying on today's playground may be tomorrow's batterer, corporate back-stabber, child abuser, or racist neighbor.

Likewise, targets of childhood peer abuse don't easily slough off the effects of bullying. Easily a quarter of my clients who show symptoms of depression or anxiety, body image problems, addictions, and relationship problems say that childhood was miserable for them due to bullying, and they associate their current problems with their childhood trauma.

Myth 6: Bullying Behavior Is Seen Only in Children

Too often, we perceive bullying as behavior that exists only among children. We ignore the reality that some adults believe they have the right to use their power to control others physically, verbally, or socially—or in other words, to bully too. We usually call adult behavior rude or inconsiderate or illegal rather than bullying. But childhood bullying exists because adult bullying exists. It's that simple. Children learn how to bully from adult role models. These role models include parents, teachers, sports and media figures, and any other adults who have an influence on children's lives. A man or woman who batters a spouse or partner or a hockey star who deliberately high-sticks an opponent is a role model for physical bullying. Yet, as with children, physical abuse is not the most common form of bullying among adults. Many adults hold prejudicial attitudes and teach children to believe that they are superior to those of a different socioeconomic, ethnic, racial, or religious group. In some adult circles, bullying is widespread and acceptable when it is camouflaged as humor in the form of prejudicial jokes.

Myth 7: Being Bullied Toughens You Up

In the disturbing results of a study of midwestern elementary school students published in 1994, a clear majority believed that not only do targets of bullying "ask for it" by being too passive, not fighting back, or acting different, but they also believe that bullying "toughens" a weak person.[6] Toughening is considered analogous to building a more positive self-concept and learning to handle the rigors of life. But, contrary to this popular belief among both children and adults, bullying doesn't toughen up anyone. Bullying is no more useful toward building a child's self-concept than being assaulted would improve an adult's self-concept. In fact, bullying of any kind does just the reverse. Targets of chronic bullying tend to be more depressed and to have lower self-esteem than do children who are not bullied. Targets also tend to show more fear and anxiety. Unless a bullied child learns appropriate assertiveness skills, he slowly loses the ability to stand up for himself.

Myth 8: Bullying Is a Rite of Passage

Bullying or being bullied—especially among adolescents—is often seen as a test to see if one can handle the perceived rigors of life. The mistaken reasoning behind this thinking is that if a young person can handle bullying—or can bully someone else—he or she is ready to take the next major step.

Most cultures throughout history have provided adolescents with some rite of passage to mark the transition between childhood and adulthood. A rite of passage, a ceremony or ritual to mark the movement from one phase of life to the next, helps the adolescent to assume the identity of a young man or young woman. We have retained some religious rites of passage, but in too many cases they have become peripheral to a young person's sense of self. For some people, graduation from high school or college, marriage, or the birth of one's first child marks the entrance into adulthood. However, because our fast-paced society doesn't support these transitional events, even these major life experiences have lost much of the significance they once held. We lack enough support for societally endorsed rites of passage, and sadly, young people seem to tacitly accept bullying to fulfill this need. One of the clearest examples of the pervasiveness of this myth is the widely accepted practice of hazing. Young people who wish to be accepted into the ranks of some military units and high school and college fraternities, sororities, and athletic organizations expect to undergo bullying. They are told they must perform humiliating and morally degrading acts or physically dangerous acts, such as drinking sometimes fatal or near-fatal amounts of alcohol. But bullying does nothing to help a young person ease into adulthood, so activities characterized by bullying behavior are not rites of passage at all.

Myth 9: Bullying Is Only the Target's Problem

Josh, a small, unathletic fifth-grader, was cornered on the playground before school by a group of fifth- and sixth-graders. They had him down on the ground, and one of the boys kicked him, while another boy threw his books aside. A handful of other kids gathered, and the air rang with shouts of "faggot" and "pussy." Some of the boys stood speechlessly and didn't join in the bullying. When a teacher heard the commotion and ran over to break it up, the kids standing around were ordered to disperse. Since it was difficult to identify who was verbally abusive, only the boys who were physically abusive were told they would need to explain their behavior to the principal, and their parents were contacted. In accordance with school policy, the boys were suspended for three days. Josh talked with the principal and was then directed to the school counselor, who after spending half an hour with him, arranged to meet on an ongoing basis twice a week to help Josh with self-esteem.

By helping Josh with his self-esteem, the school personnel felt that the problem was effectively resolved, but it wasn't— they had neglected to deal with the emotional needs of the others involved in the incident. In this case, as in many bullying incidents, most of the attention is focused on helping the target of bullying, but attention also needs to be paid to the other victims of bullying—the bystanders and the instigators.

In the average school, 60 percent of the students are not directly involved in bullying incidents as chronic targets or instigators but are bystanders who witness bullying.[7] Adults usually overlook bystanders, but they are deeply affected, too. Bystanders often say they'd like to do something, but don't know what to do and fear that they, too, will be attacked. Though they may not have actively taken part, they feel as if they are party to the abuse and are guilt-stricken for not intervening. This guilt and confusion can negatively affect their self-esteem, and bystanders often feel victimized. Standing by while someone else is abused can also lead to desensitization and a sense of powerlessness, making it even less likely that observers will intervene in future bullying encounters. Unfortunately, another danger of witnessing bullying is that bystanders become themselves more likely to bully. To confront these negative affects, adults need to encourage bystanders to speak out against bullying, to do what they can to protect peers who have difficulty standing up for themselves, and to report peer abuse to school authorities when preventive actions haven't worked.

In most instances, the needs of children who bully are also dismissed. Instigators are usually punished for their misbehavior, but they don't often get the emotional help they need to change their attitudes of superiority and entitlement. As a result, children who bully encounter long-term problems. They are more likely to drop out of high school. As adults, they stand a greater chance of having dysfunctional relationships, of abusing their own children, and of being incarcerated.

What We Can Do

Violence occurs when people actively or passively condone intolerance. We need to examine how we perpetuate these myths about bullying. It is the responsibility of adults to create a world in which children learn the values of empathy, peacemaking, and acceptance through an active rejection of the myths surrounding bullying.

Next we'll consider some practical ideas to confront the societal attitudes that reinforce bullying. These are general ways that we can help all children. You'll find the specific suggestions and how-to's for helping your child in the chapters to follow.

Take Personal Responsibility for Creating a World of Nonviolence

Too often we don't admit our own potentials for being violent. Tolerating violence makes us accomplices to violence, if not direct participants. We blame others for violence in the world, shifting the responsibility for change onto someone else. We know that the effects of childhood peer abuse can follow targets and instigators alike into adulthood, that adults are responsible for modeling much of the bullying we see in children, and that bullying affects not only the target, but also bystanders, instigators, and the larger community. By confronting these myths, we empower ourselves to create a culture that leaves less room for violence.

At a conference on combating school violence through peacemaking at which Dr. Arun Gandhi, grandson of Mahatma Gandhi, spoke, an attendee commented that Gandhi was singing to the choir—that this crowd of educators, therapists, and helping professionals didn't need to hear any more on the value of nonviolence or on being nonviolent *themselves*. What they needed to hear was how to help *other people—the troublemakers*—learn the value of nonviolence.

Dr. Gandhi pointed out that this common attitude is part of the problem. Striving to be peaceful people ourselves is how we create a more peaceful world. Recognizing our own tendencies toward violence and working diligently to change ourselves into more peaceful people takes constant work, but we must do this work if we hope to eliminate our own inadvertent contributions to societal violence. To create a more compassionate world, we must challenge ourselves and others to assume responsibility for our part.

Challenge Your Stereotypes

Become aware of the ways in which you stereotype people. Listen not only to how you speak about others, but how you think about them. Many of the stereotypes we hold are invisible even to ourselves until we make a conscious effort to pay attention. What are the assumptions you hold about people of other races? Different ethnic origins? People of other religions? Homosexual people? Heterosexual people? Professionals? Blue-collar workers? Welfare parents? By challenging the ways we stereotype others, we are confronting all of the bullying myths by choosing to honor all people with dignity.

Be honest with yourself about the stereotypes you hold and the assumptions you make about others. Ask yourself why you hold those beliefs, and work to consciously confront them if they are destructive, elitist, or bigoted. Don't allow yourself to accept them with "That's the way I was raised." Many of us have had stereotypes drummed into our heads since we were young and were taught to look down on others for all sorts of irrational and unjustifiable reasons.

One of the most common ways we show stereotypical thinking is through racist, sexist, ageist, homophobic, or religiously intolerant jokes. Such jokes are a form of verbal bullying. When we tell them or allow them to pass unchallenged, the bullying is normalized and the subject of the jokes is dehumanized. How often do we squirm in discomfort because we know we should say something to an adult telling derogatory jokes?

Challenge the Use of Physical Discipline

When we challenge the use of physical discipline, we acknowledge that bullying is more than just a children's problem. Rarely a week goes by in my office without at least one parent telling me, "What most of these kids need is a good whack on the butt!" They complain that we're losing control of our kids because not enough parents are using physical discipline. I ask them to think about the meaning of the word *discipline*, which comes from the same Latin root as does *disciple*, meaning "to learn." If the purpose of discipline is to teach, what are we teaching through physical punishment?

Spanking, hitting, or slapping children teaches them to fear the person doing the violence, but more disturbingly, violent punishment teaches children to become violent themselves. Perhaps the primary reason we have a problem with bullying among children, as well as with adults who are violent, is that we allow adults to use their power to harm children. Study after study shows that when children are exposed to harsh corporal (physical) punishment, they are more likely to be violent with their peers. Physically disciplined children have learned that the way to deal with frustration and conflict is to strike out physically. Children who are raised with *nonphysical* discipline are more considerate and more likely to show empathy toward others than children who are raised with physical discipline.

We must work to change the attitude that parents can physically discipline children in the name of love. We cannot consider ourselves actively engaged in rejecting the myths about bullying as long as we consider it acceptable for parents to regard physical discipline as an appropriate part of childrearing.

We must be more creative in our problem-solving skills if we want to break the bullying cycle.

Challenge Toxic Media

By acknowledging the toxicity of intolerance and gratuitous violence in the media, we are actively confronting the myth that bullying behavior is seen only in children. According to Thomas Aquinas, there are two types of books—those that will help lead you to God, and those that won't. The same could be said of modern media, and whether it will lead to a world of nonviolence. In an ideal world, adults would create materials for the media that would promote compassion, acceptance, and peace. Instead, children are exposed constantly to offensive language and depictions of graphic violence. Theorists continue to debate whether the media tends to *create* a more violent culture or simply *reflects* the tendencies toward violence that already exist. I believe it's a little of both.

We can look at violence and coarseness in the media as a symptom of a deeper societal disease. We should be seriously troubled by a culture whose media minimizes and even degrades kindness toward others. In a magazine review of *There's Something about Mary,* the writer raved, saying the movie had a "refreshing mean-spiritedness." Why should we welcome mean-spiritedness in our movies? We see this same celebration of cruelty and intolerance in many popular television shows.

Some depictions of violence are necessary or useful to tell a coherent and socially valuable story. Although movies like *Schindler's List* and *Saving Private Ryan* aren't appropriate for young children who haven't reached the developmental level necessary to understand the message, older children can learn important lessons about compassion from movies that deglorify violence.

Peace researcher, educator, and representative to the United Nations Betty Reardon describes violence as "a failure of the imagination."[8] Nowhere is this more true than in the media. We need to deal imaginatively with the social problems that confront us. Most American adults want the media cleaned up, but desire isn't enough. We must confront gratuitous meanness, cruelty, and sexual exploitation in the media.

Make it your business to know what your children are hearing, viewing, reading, and playing, and don't allow music, television, books, magazines, videos, or video games that you consider offensive in your home. If you find something offensive, this can be a wonderful opportunity for you to share your values with your child. For example, you can read the lyrics of a song together, and then explain why you find them offensive. Try not to lecture, but instead really listen to your child's opinions, while still holding a firm moral ground. Make clear, understandable guidelines about what's acceptable and adhere to them. Some would say this makes martyrs of the banned media figures or materials, making them even more desirable, but I disagree. That's like saying, "Kids are going to smoke pot anyway, so I'd rather let them smoke at home so they don't have to hide it." But children need to be able to develop within the freedom of healthy limits. Research shows that not setting limits for children can lead to delinquency, drug abuse, and antisocial behavior. Parents must take a stand on what is and is not acceptable.

Challenge Gossip

By actively confronting the ways in which we maliciously gossip, we are challenging the myth that bullying is just playing around. Gossiping is a national pastime. Just take a look at the tabloids in any supermarket checkout lane or listen to the talk shows that sensationalize people's problems and cheapen human relationships.

Gossip doesn't solve anything, and it alienates people. Malicious gossip is relational bullying. Children have learned much about verbal and relational peer abuse by observing their parents. When adults gossip, they give children the message that it's acceptable to put down someone who does not have the opportunity to respond. The prevalence of gossip proves that bullying is not something people naturally outgrow. It takes an ongoing commitment to refuse to gossip and to dismantle this part of society's bullying machinery.

When tempted to gossip, ask yourself why you want to discuss someone who's not there. Is it because you want to feel vindicated because someone has offended you? Do you want to feel superior to them? Do you have something to say that would be better said to them? People deserve the dignity of privacy. Refuse to take part in gossip and pass this value to your children by making your home a strict no-gossip zone.

3

The Impact of Bullying on Children

A wealth of research conducted during the past two decades has produced shocking revelations about the impact of bullying on children's lives. Dan Olweus, a psychologist from the University of Bergen in Norway, was a pioneer researcher in examining how bullying affected children. He found far-reaching benefits for all students when antibullying programs reduced aggressive behaviors in schools. Not only did a reduction in bullying lead to a lower incidence of violence, but school morale was enhanced, truancy was reduced, and overall academic performance improved.[1] Olweus's research created a global groundswell of interest in peer abuse.

In her groundbreaking book *The Nurture Assumption,* Judith Rich Harris argues compellingly that childhood peers are much more influential in shaping our personalities than we are aware. "Low status in the peer group, if it continues for long," writes Harris, "leaves permanent marks on the personality. And it can sure wreck a kid's childhood."[2] There's no question about it. Targets of bullying often suffer low status, and childhood can feel like a constant uphill struggle.

Although Harris is referring here primarily to targets, children who bully are also severely affected by their behavior.

How Bullying Affects Targets

When Nathaniel was six years old, he was in a tragic automobile accident that almost claimed his life. After the accident, he underwent numerous operations that required months of recuperation. He could not participate in normal play for several years after the accident, and a group of boys began to call him a sissy and—what hurt even worse—"Frankenstein" because he walked with a slight limp. A chubby boy, he was dubbed "Fat Nat." Though he was never physically assaulted, the taunts took a major toll on his self-confidence because he didn't assert himself against the verbal abuse. His tormentors called him a wimp, and subsequently Nathaniel began to think of himself as less masculine than the other boys. Even though most of the other children didn't pester him, they'd stand around and watch as Nathaniel was called names, and no one ever stepped in to intervene or help him.

In sixth grade, Nathaniel's doctors gave him a clean bill of health and told him he could do anything the other boys were doing. Football tryouts were coming up, and as much as he wanted to play and be a part of what the other boys did, there was no way he'd submit himself to their ridicule. He gave up his football dream—something that would undoubtedly have helped his self-concept—and continued to avoid the boys who harassed him.

Nathaniel finally took a risk and tried out for soccer in his freshman year. He made the team but remembers the humiliation he felt when the girl spectators laughed at him each time he ran down the field because his stomach bulged out of his jersey. His self-concept was tied to being laughed at—he felt that he would always be an unlikable, wimpy, fat kid.

After high school, he decided he'd had enough of being

humiliated and started working out at a gym. He noticed that as the pounds came off, women started paying attention. Yet, he remembered the taunts of his childhood peers and still thought of himself as a wimpy fat kid. He was on constant guard around men and women, afraid to be considered ridiculous by women and unassertive and therefore unmasculine by men.

Now twenty-eight years old and married for three years, Nathaniel is strikingly handsome with an easygoing manner that belies the fact that he suffered from peer abuse a decade earlier. But he has been sorely damaged. Nathaniel is a sex addict and has had eight affairs since his wedding day. He found that he could temporarily relieve his nagging self-doubts about his attractiveness and masculinity by sexual promiscuity.

Like Nathaniel, most children will be confronted by aggressive peers in their early school years. The way they handle the first few confrontations at a new school or with a new instigator affects the way children who bully will react to them in the future. A child who handles these initial situations successfully is not likely to be bullied any further. However, instigators of bullying will see a child who has difficulty being assertive as vulnerable and as someone who can be singled out as a target. Even though a child may do her best to deal with the situation, the longer bullying goes on with no relief, the more discouraged, fearful, and helpless the child will feel, until she is convinced that nothing will ever be any different. This sort of discouragement leads to a sense of hopelessness and to a variety of problems that can extend into adulthood.

Intrapersonal Problems

Because they feel cheated and trapped in a vicious circle over which they feel little control, chronic targets of bullying usually have low self-confidence and often suffer from clinical depression throughout childhood. Their depression can often lead to even greater feelings of isolation. Embarrassed and ashamed, they may not to want to talk about their feelings with anyone. The more isolated a child feels, the more depressed he becomes. Targets of peer abuse are also more likely to have thoughts of suicide and to make attempts at suicide.

Chronic targets of bullying also tend to have more than their share of anxiety problems, as well. *Anxiety* means any abnormal fear or worry that gets in the way of normal functioning. Of course, all children worry from time to time, and many fears are rational. It makes sense to fear someone who bullies. Who wouldn't? This natural fear often leads to a realistic assessment of the problem and encourages the target to find ways to handle it. However, when that fear becomes crippling anxiety, it adversely affects the child's life. Symptoms of anxiety may include sleeplessness, nightmares, tics or nervous habits, and refusal to go to school. Physical symptoms, such as poor appetite, gastrointestinal problems, and dermatological problems are common. Targets of bullying are three to four times more likely than nontargets to have problems with insomnia, anxiety, and severe depression.[3] Austin, a ten-year-old boy with a learning disability, became so fearful of his classmate Brian's daily taunts that he developed eczema, woke up in the morning with stomachaches, and eventually refused to go to school.

Emotional problems spawned by childhood peer abuse don't always stop in childhood, and they can go on to affect adults. Many who felt isolated and depressed as children because of peer abuse continue to feel that way as adults. In my experience with clients, clinical depression and anxiety-related problems, such as social phobias, are common for adult survivors of peer abuse.

Interpersonal Problems

Children who are chronically bullied usually don't know how to defend themselves with words. Very often, the child who bullies is more powerful verbally and is quicker with comebacks and put-downs, and the target doesn't know how to respond. Once a belittling label, like wimp, wuss, queer, freak, or hag, is attached to a target, it becomes very difficult for the child to get rid of it. Names like these are meant to keep the target in a vulnerable position and to depersonalize the child. This is intimidating and shaming, especially if others are present. Consequently, many targets of bullying go out of their way to avoid their attackers and the places they frequent. Anxiety and fear are constants because school is considered an unsafe and unpleasant place. A study published in 1994 shows that up to 7 percent of U.S. eighth-graders stay home at least once a month because they fear emotional or physical attack by aggressive students.[4]

Shyness, an inborn trait, is a common attribute of targets of peer abuse. Shy children are more vulnerable than others to being bullied, and being the target of bullying exacerbates the problem of natural shyness. Shy children suffer when their natural timidity is compounded by feelings of shame and intimidation.

Shy or not, many targets become preoccupied with thoughts of revenge against their attackers. Most bullied children never act out their anger. Yet it's no simple coincidence that so many perpetrators of school violence have been targets of chronic bullying at school. Prolonged peer abuse creates profound rage in some children, and some choose to fight back with a vengeance. The fear and lack of self-confidence a target feels can be enduring and can last well into adulthood, affecting them in various negative ways. In my clinical practice, I've observed that men and women who experienced childhood peer abuse tend to fear intimacy in relationships.

Many adults who were bullied as children also have problems making friends, making ordinary conversation, and feeling relaxed in social situations like parties or in work environments.

Academic Problems

Kids who are worrying about being abused can't study. Even though many targets of bullying have a positive attitude toward schoolwork, their work suffers because coping with the emotional pain of bullying consumes their energy. Worrying about when the next verbal or physical assault may take place makes it difficult for the child to concentrate and focus on tasks.

Jackie, a shy and intelligent fifth-grader, loves all of her subjects in school, but lately her grades have been dropping. She can't concentrate after lunch because she spends so much of her time worrying about an eighth-grader who harasses her on the bus about her developing breasts. She fears telling her parents or school authorities because the boy has a reputation for being violent, and she is afraid the abuse could get worse. Meanwhile, her grades continue to suffer.

Many students report the main reason they get bullied is because they do well in school. Many of the kids labeled as "geeks" or "nerds" will courageously suffer through school and make valuable contributions to society as adults. But not always. Sometimes bullying will induce students to leave school for good even if they are above average students. Ten percent of high school dropouts say that they didn't return because of their fear of being harassed or attacked.[5]

Substance Abuse Problems

It's no surprise that the stress experienced by targets of bullying can result in significant problems with substance abuse. An easy way for kids who are targeted to fit in is to start using tobacco, alcohol, or other drugs because it's "cool" among some peer groups. Children who start using substances as a way to be accepted may then continue to use them to temporarily escape their emotional pain. This puts a young person at great risk of becoming chemically dependent, because the younger a child is when he or she first uses alcohol or other drugs, the greater the chance of becoming addicted.

How Bullying Affects Children Who Bully

Troy recalls how in the second grade he enjoyed placing lit firecrackers in the mouths of frogs, then watching them hop off and explode. He laughs as he recounts having spent more time in the principal's office than in the classroom. Usually, he was called in for fighting, but he was wily enough never to get caught harassing other kids. He smiles and tells how he mercilessly taunted one boy in a wheelchair whom he called "Metal Man," until the target's parents finally pulled their son from the school.

Troy remembers being very popular through elementary and middle school. "Those kids respected me," he said, "because I didn't take any shit from anybody. I still don't." Like many children who bully, Troy confused fear with respect. In his freshman year of high school, he joined the G's, a violent youth gang whose initiation required that he either participate in a gang rape or steal a car. He chose to rape a girl he didn't know from another school and was admitted to the gang.

As a sophomore, Troy was expelled from school for carrying a weapon and didn't return. For a few years, he found easy money dealing drugs. "I can always go back to that," he quips as he stares through the bars of his cell in the state prison, where he is serving a sentence for armed robbery.

Unfortunately, Troy's story is all too common. Helping children discontinue bullying behaviors when they are young is critical, as this startling statistic testifies: Children who are identified in the second grade as instigators of bullying are a whopping six times more likely than those who don't bully to be convicted of a crime by age twenty-four, and five times more likely to have a serious criminal record by age thirty.[6] Clearly, the outlook for children who bully is not bright. As bullying behaviors become more and more entrenched, aggression and lack of empathy for others become habitual and lead to serious lifelong problems with relationships, careers, and the legal system. Children who bully tend to externalize, meaning they blame others for the problems they themselves cause. They do not see that their own attitudes and behaviors are causing them problems.

Not long ago, I witnessed a textbook example of externalizing. I was at an elementary school when a student walking down the hall came across a maintenance man who was on a ladder. The boy stood there a moment, then asked the man on the ladder, "Hey, mister, what would you think if I shook your ladder?"

"I would not appreciate that, son. Please don't."

The boy then grabbed the ladder and shook it, causing the man to lose his balance and fall. Fortunately he was not injured. He immediately took the boy to the principal's office. The boy's parents were called and he was given an in-school suspension as punishment. When the boy crossed paths with the maintenance man later that day, the youngster glared and said, "You got me in trouble." Characteristic of a child who bullies, the boy did not accept responsibility for his behavior but instead chose to blame the person he targeted.

This attitude can develop into chronic problems for children who bully. Manipulation, deception, lying, and getting away with things become a way of life. We hear the litany of excuses that children who bully use to absolve themselves of personal responsibility: "He asked for it." "Why are you always blaming me?" "It wasn't my fault!"

The inner messages that dominate a bullying child's life, such as "I am superior to you, so I treat you how I choose to," generate predictable problems intrapersonally, interpersonally, academically, vocationally, and legally.

Intrapersonal Problems

The inner life of a child who bullies is often marked by turmoil. As I've already mentioned, many of these girls and boys tend to be angrier, more depressed, more impulsive, and more likely to feel that they don't belong at school. Many children who bully are clinically depressed but often do not receive treatment for their depression, which goes unnoticed because adults are more concerned with the immediate problem of controlling their behavior. It's easy to understand why many children who bully are depressed. The show of false bravado we often see with these children is a cover-up for a profound sense of inner emptiness, inadequacy, and feeling unloved. Children who bully are often in denial of feelings based in shame and anger. Recognizing and admitting such pain and vulnerability is difficult, and one of the greatest and most damaging fears for these children is the fear of asking anyone for help with their problems.

Interpersonal Problems

While Andy is standing at the bus stop, he thinks about a science experiment the class had conducted that day. He looks absently in the direction of a group of kids, from which Joe emerges to confront him. "Are you staring at me?" Joe snarls. Andy replies that he wasn't staring, he was just thinking to himself. Shoving Andy backward and knocking him down, Joe shouts so everyone else can hear, "Don't ever stare at me again, punk."

Like Joe, children who bully characteristically see hostile intent where there is none, which often leads them to react to situations aggressively and inappropriately. They often have great difficulty restraining their emotions. Many times these children are quicker to act out in anger and have greater trouble controlling their anger than most children. But not all children who bully fit this description. Sometimes children who bully are cool and detached and aren't prone to react brashly to perceived threats. Instead, these children will wait for opportunities to bully when they know adults or peers who would be likely to stop them won't catch them. Either pattern of behavior can lead to lifelong problems and result in children who bully being more likely to be involved in violent crimes as adults.

All children who bully, however, show a lack of empathy, which is critical in the development of healthy relationships. To really enjoy closeness with others, we have to care about how they feel and how our behavior affects them. But children who bully don't feel the same sense of remorse after hurting someone that most people feel, so difficulties with friendships often develop as the bullying child grows older.

In the early grades, this child can be quite popular. He is able to get what he wants when he wants it, and he may have a following of kids who admire him because of the power he wields. As adolescence comes on, however, popularity drops off. What used to be seen as "cool" is now seen as annoying and immature. Children who have learned the value of getting along, cooperating, and treating each other with respect gravitate toward one another. The bullying child, who is often regarded with disdain, is seen more and more as someone to avoid. This narrows the choice of friends for children who bully. By senior high school, if still attending school, an aggressive child will usually have peer relationships with children who reinforce his or her status, and often these individuals will be other children who bully. In the worst-case scenario, the adolescent has become involved in gangs.

Despite apparent self-confidence, the child who bullies has a very tenuous hold on self-esteem. Although studies do indicate that children who bully for the most part will say they like who they are,[7] they feel good about themselves only to the degree that they can feel a sense of superiority over others. It's as if they are saying, "I am only OK to the degree that I can control you." Children who bully typically feel an underlying sense of inadequacy, and they use power and control over others to avoid thinking about their own inadequacy. The more unloved, inadequate, and inferior the child feels, the more difficult it is to accept these feelings, face them, and deal with them. Instead of confronting these deep-seated fears directly, the child who bullies uses a psychological defense mechanism called *projection*. With projection, one's own unwanted feelings or characteristics are overlaid on someone else. The child who bullies essentially says, "I know I'm not inferior (or unloved, or inadequate) because *you* are, and I'm better than you."

The child who bullies has little insight into who she really is, and meaningful interactions with others become extremely difficult, especially as the child moves into adolescence. As other children are developing empathy and self-insight, the lack of insight for the child who bullies becomes a serious problem. The deeper the sense of inadequacy such children feel, the more they will act out against peers. All their interactions are motivated by the need to keep a sense of personal dignity and to make themselves appear important.

If these children reach adulthood without resolving the often unconscious sense of inadequacy that motivates bullying, they'll continue to seek superiority and control in relationships to mask these deep feelings. They run a much greater risk of having dysfunctional family relationships and problems with domestic violence. Raising children requires patience, the ability and willingness to empathize, and an ability to handle anger and frustration. As instigators of bullying reach adulthood and have their own children, they are more likely to abuse them. When one or both parents were aggressive as children, their own children are more likely to exhibit bullying behavior.

Academic, Vocational, and Legal Problems

Children who bully tend to set lower academic and vocational goals for themselves than do other children. Children who bully are more likely to have a negative attitude toward schoolwork, and as time goes on, they are more likely to underachieve academically and to drop out of school. Adults who instigated bullying as children are likely to have fewer years of education and to earn less than those who did not. As a result, these adults tend to be more dissatisfied with their adult careers because the goals they set are below their potential. Again, as is typical of these individuals, they tend to blame external circumstances rather than to examine how their own attitudes and choices brought them to their current situation.

Instigators of bullying are more likely than other adolescents to be involved with vandalism, fighting, theft, drunkenness, and truancy and to have an arrest by young adulthood.[8] Involvement with the legal system may continue throughout adulthood. For instance, it's been found that adult men who bullied as children had more numerous criminal convictions, and for more severe crimes, as well as more traffic violations and convictions for drunk driving, than those who were not instigators of peer abuse as children.[9]

Children are obviously affected by peer abuse differently, depending on whether they are targets or instigators of bullying. Yet there is hope for all children affected by bullying, especially when parents are willing to work with them. We can help our children past the rocky shores of childhood by helping targets and instigators of bullying learn to value themselves for the unique people they are. Only then can they navigate the seas of adulthood without being weighed down by the anchors of childhood pain.

WHAT TO DO IF YOUR CHILD IS A TARGET OF BULLYING

4

How to Know If Your Child Is Being Bullied

Though many children are very vocal with their parents about bullying, it's often difficult for some children to talk with *anyone* about what's happening because they feel ashamed, weak, inadequate, unsure, or fearful. A young child is more likely than an older child to see a parent as someone who can help stop the abuse and is thus more likely to talk to a parent about bullying. By the time a child is in middle school, he is less likely to spontaneously tell a parent about problems with peer abuse.

If you notice a big change in your child's normal behavior, you may want to investigate whether the cause is bullying. Say, for instance, that your normally high-energy child appears depressed or your normally relaxed child acts wound up—you'd want to know if they are reacting to bullying behavior. Whether or not children open up to parents about bullying on their own, it's important for parents to recognize some common warning signs that their child might be a target of bullying.

Warning Signs

If your child shows any of the following signs, he or she may be a target of bullying:

- Any change in normal behavior
- Reluctance to attend school or peer-centered activities at school
- Unexplainable drop in academic performance
- Torn clothing
- Headaches, stomachaches, or other unexplainable illnesses
- Waking frequently, sleeping more than normal, or other changes in sleep patterns
- Avoiding peers and social groupings at school
- Avoiding the school cafeteria or playground
- Avoiding extracurricular activities
- Loss of interest in activities formerly enjoyed
- Sad and depressed demeanor
- Reluctance to walk to or from school
- Reluctance to talk about what's happening at school

Children who bully like to pick on the easiest targets, and some children are more likely to become targets because of the way they behave. Targets' behavior can be either passive or provocative.

Passive Targets of Bullying

Submissive children, those kids who have difficulty being assertive, are the most likely to be chronic targets of children who bully. On some level, most unassertive children understand that the real reason instigators target them is not because of the way they look, whether or not they're smart, or the brand of shoes they wear. They know that their inability to defend themselves from attack attracts children who bully. Some children have a harder time being assertive than others. Shy children, traumatized children, and physically weak or smaller children often have trouble being assertive with children who bully, and they need some coaching in what to do when faced with aggressive peers. The responses of nonassertive children in the following examples reveal how a little training in assertiveness skills could turn around their lives.

Shy Children

Tania, a third-grader, has always been a shy, quiet girl. As an only child, she spends much of her time with her parents and their adult friends and feels quite comfortable with them. But she lacks the social skills to make friends with peers. She rarely talks with others at school unless they talk with her first, and she often spends playground time alone. This week Kylie, a popular classmate, invited all the girls to her birthday party except Tania, whom Kylie said was "weird." Tania felt bad that she wasn't invited, but didn't say anything to anyone until her parents, who noticed that she was quieter than usual and even seemed a little depressed, were able to draw her out.

Most children feel shy from time to time. They will often have trouble meeting someone for the first time, going places where they don't know anyone, saying or doing something that makes them appear different, or being teased. But children who can be considered "shy" feel uncomfortable in social situations almost constantly. A shy child's nervousness around others stems from a fear of being embarrassed or humiliated. These children feel anxiety when separated from their parents, fail to make eye contact in social situations, and feel uncomfortable with groups of peers.

Traumatized Children

When Timothy was ten years old, he saw his parents and older brother die in an automobile accident. He moved to a different state to live with relatives and has had difficulty making the adjustment. Now a quiet, withdrawn sixth-grader, Timothy shows signs of depression and post-traumatic stress disorder (PTSD). He has frequent nightmares, fears riding in cars, and neglects his personal hygiene. When other kids call him "Smelly" and other names because he hasn't bathed, he often runs away or starts to cry.

A variety of painful events, including accidents, natural disasters, parents' divorce, abuse, chronic family stress, or having witnessed a violent crime, may traumatize a child. Unresolved trauma can affect a child in profound ways, leading to serious emotional problems, such as PTSD. Such children, often overcome with anxiety and fear, are unable to function in ways that would help them be included in peer activities. They may be seen as "oversensitive" because their feelings are easily hurt. To protect themselves from further pain, they may avoid social contact with other children. This distancing makes them even more susceptible to bullying.

Physically Weak or Small Children

Luke, a second-grader, is small for his age. He doesn't know how to stand up for himself when Travis calls him "Foureyes" and pushes him around on the playground as other kids in his class watch. He feels embarrassed and angry, hunches his shoulders and crosses his arms, but doesn't say anything. A couple of other boys join in, and the taunts rise to a chorus. The bell rings, and Luke is saved again by the bell. He wishes Travis and his friends would stop harassing him and be nice, but he knows they won't. It will happen again tomorrow.

Although a child's size or strength is often not the real problem, a child who is smaller or physically weaker than peers may be more likely to be targets of bullying. Small or weak children who are bullied often have poor body images. Boys' self-images are closely connected to physical strength, and boys are targeted because of small stature and low physical strength more often than are girls.

Provocative Targets of Bullying

Some children seem to ask to be bullied. They'll egg on a child who bullies and then threaten to tell the teacher, or they may go out of their way to do something they know the child who bullies doesn't like. They'll walk right by a group of kids who they know are trouble, like moths drawn to a flame. These children elicit little sympathy from teachers and other students because to shed their roles as targets, they just have to *stop* doing something. But they either don't want to stop—which is understandably annoying to teachers—or they don't seem to be able to stop.

Children who provoke other students into bullying are called *provocative targets*. They share characteristics of both instigators and targets. It's difficult to identify them as targets because we often perceive them as instigators of a bullying situation. A provocative target will fall into one of three categories but will often exhibit some characteristics from the other categories as well. These categories are: attention seekers, stimulation seekers, and revenge seekers.

Attention Seekers

Abe is a fourth-grader whose favorite T-shirt displays a Tasmanian Devil cartoon character, an uncannily appropriate symbol for Abe's behavior in school. Although Abe would never consider hassling anyone weaker, therefore not qualifying as a child who bullies, he can't resist bothering boys who bully and whom he knows will take his bait. Abe's regular routine includes running up behind Jorge, a burly fifth-grader, calling him names, and then trying to outrun the boy after he loses his patience. Like a pesky fly, Abe annoys others, but he picks only boys who he knows are going to get the better of him. Abe often gets caught and winds up losing fights, at which time he complains to the principal, "He started it." The consequence of Abe's poor social skills is that he has no close friends. He has a desperate need to be noticed and finds that negative attention is better than no attention at all.

Attention seekers are so needy that they are willing to do almost anything for attention. Other children usually find them immature and don't want to associate with them. The only option attention seekers can think of to get noticed is to seek negative attention from children who bully. Unfortunately, they get themselves in over their heads and often wind up getting hurt.

Stimulation Seekers

Dominic is a third-grade student who has been diagnosed with attention-deficit/hyperactivity disorder (AD/HD). He often complains of being bored, has a hard time sitting still, has difficulty sharing and taking turns in games with other children, and acts impulsively. Like many provocative targets, Dominic has a hard time anticipating the consequences of his behavior. He acts before he thinks.

Dominic gets emotionally upset and easily frustrated, and when he is irritated, he is just as likely to take his anger out on a child who bullies as on anyone else. He doesn't stop to think that his misdirected anger could get him in trouble, and it often does. He can't figure out why he ends up on the losing end of his interactions with peers.

All provocative targets act impulsively, but stimulation seekers are more impulsive than most. Many provocative targets are diagnosed with AD/HD. Children with AD/HD feel as if they have "information overload" and attempt to discharge energy by acting out.

Revenge Seekers

A reserved girl, Rebecca is self-conscious about her appearance. She has struggled with her self-image because of an ongoing and considerable weight problem, and to compound matters, she has developed a severe case of facial acne over the past year. Rebecca has been tormented by the same group of girls at school since fourth grade, and now that she is in seventh grade, she's decided she's had enough. Rebecca feels that the teachers ignore her pleas for help, claiming she's old enough to deal with the problems on her own, and she has grown tired of at least two teachers' attitudes that she is being a "whining crybaby." In addition, she believes her physical education teacher, an attractive and vivacious young woman, looks down on her and favors girls who aren't overweight.

Lately Rebecca has started to leave nasty notes for several of her tormentors, implying that they are lesbian and sexually active with each other. One day after last-period gym class, the girls find her alone dressing in the locker room, take all of her school and gym clothes, and toss them in the garbage outside school. A female custodian finds Rebecca crying in the shower room several hours later.

Rebecca is a typical provocative target whose motive is revenge against the children who have been harassing her. Although Rebecca hasn't sought revenge against the teachers who haven't helped her, many revenge seekers do act out against adults or bystanders who haven't provided support. Unfortunately, revenge-seeking provocative targets generally only complicate an already painful and difficult situation.

If your child tells you about bullying, if you notice warning signs, or if your child seems to be either a passive or provocative target, your next step is to learn how to talk with your child to resolve the problem.

5

Talking with Your Child about Bullying

Nothing hurts like seeing your child in pain, particularly when the pain is due to something as cruel and unfair as bullying. Remember that what your child needs most is for you to listen respectfully, not for you to solve the problem. Your child needs to know that there are effective and nonviolent ways to deal with bullying, and that you're going to teach him those skills. We'll talk about skills in detail in chapters 6 and 7, but the focus of this chapter is to examine your reaction to discovering your child's situation and to give you the skills to talk with him.

As much as peer abuse can affect a child's sense of self-worth, children can become adept at hiding the fact that they're being bullied if they're afraid that a parent would make the situation worse by talking with the bullying child or her parents.

Though it's not always the case, children who are frequent targets of bullying often have overprotective parents. Overprotectiveness is an overreaction to the normal parental wish to keep a child safe. Protecting a child from dangers or stresses with which the child is unable to cope is an important part of parenting. But protecting a child from normal life situations and stress, such as bullying that doesn't pose a serious threat to the child, gives the message that the child is incapable of handling these situations on his own. Over-protectiveness, though done out of love and good intentions, leads a child to feel insecure, anxious, and weak. The more overprotective a parent is, the more fearful and less confident the child is likely to be. See whether you can imagine yourself overreacting like the parents in the following scenarios of over-protective parenting:

Scenario 1

Recently, a seventh-grade boy acts depressed and has been spending most of his time alone in his room. His father suspects bullying because he heard a couple of neighborhood boys call his son a geek and a nerd when his son got off the bus. Because his son has always been quiet and sensi-tive, his father fears he can't handle the verbal abuse. At supper he tells his son what he heard the boys say, and that he would start driving him to and from school every day. The boy agreed and felt relieved, yet he knew his father's intervention wouldn't help when the boys verbally abused him at school. He also felt even more inadequate and weak because his father didn't have enough faith in him to deal with the problem.

By rescuing his son, this father was teaching him to avoid problems, not to deal with them assertively. Discussing the bullying would give his boy a clear message of confidence in his abilities to find a solution and would have been a better approach.

Scenario 2

A new girl at school calls an overweight fourth-grade girl "Porky." The girl, who has never encountered peer abuse before, comes home in tears. Upon hearing the details, her mother storms off to the girl's house to speak with her and her parents.

By taking over her daughter's situation, this mother is depriving her daughter of an opportunity to explore her feelings about the abuse and to find a way to deal with it if it happens again. It would have been more helpful to talk with her daughter about how she felt and to brainstorm some solutions.

Reasons for Overprotectiveness

Overprotectiveness often develops out of a parent's own unresolved childhood issues. You may feel compelled to be overprotective if any of the following is true for you:

- You were bullied as a child.
- You are easily offended and have difficulty with being assertive when someone hurts your feelings.
- Your own parents were overprotective.
- You were taught it's not "nice" to be assertive.
- You were a very fearful or timid child.

Some clear guidelines will help you determine if you are being appropriately protective or overprotective. A parent is overprotective if he or she engages in any of the following behaviors:

- Routinely does things for the child that the child is capable of doing
- Acts as if the child is younger than the child really is and is therefore incapable of handling age-appropriate situations

- Treats the child as emotionally incapable to deal with any stressful situation
- Intervenes when the bullied child, who is not being physically harmed or threatened and shows no signs of psychological harm, has asked the parent not to intervene

Responding Effectively

If your child is in physical danger, parental intervention is necessary. Danger to psychological well-being can be just as serious as physical danger, and parents need to decide whether to intervene in a case of verbal or relational bullying. If peer abuse continues to be a pattern after your child has done everything he can to stop it, intervention is usually appropriate. Once you've checked your initial reaction and impulses after learning that your child is being bullied, you need to communicate with your child in a way that encourages openness. This requires that you be calm, really listen, be supportive, accept your child's feelings, and help your child determine possible solutions. If you think your child may provoke bullying, you need to ask questions that will help you determine what's behind this behavior.

Be Calm

When deciding upon a course of action, you must remember to stay calm. Naturally, it's hard to be calm when your child is being hurt emotionally or physically. You may want to storm out to find the bullying child's parents, tell them off, and settle the score. Worse yet, you may want to find the bullying child and do the same. Angry feelings are understandable, but irrational, hasty action will probably compound the problem.

Despite your anger, you must express your feelings clearly and nonjudgmentally. Your job is to teach your child that you believe in her, and a calm, interested demeanor is the best way to go about that. When talking with your child, don't put down or apply labels to the bullying child. In fact, don't even call the child doing the bullying a bully. Call the child by his or her name instead. Make it clear that no one has a right to mistreat another person and that the child who is bullying is wrong to mistreat your child, but do not model aggressive behavior yourself. The skills on assertiveness presented in the next chapter, skills you'll be teaching your child, will help you keep calm in this trying situation.

The following example shows how you could calmly respond if your child has been physically bullied: "I feel very angry with Joey for hitting you like he did, and I feel sad that you were treated like that. Let's see what we can do to figure out some ways to deal with Joey."

Sometimes it can be helpful to share a real-life experience of bullying that was targeted at you and that you handled successfully. This incident could have occurred either in childhood or adulthood, though it is easier for a child to relate to a childhood incident. Sharing in this way helps your child to feel less alone with the problem and to feel that you really understand.

One mother shared with her daughter her own experience of verbal bullying: "I feel sad that Jane called you fat. I also feel angry with Jane that she treated you that way. You seem like you really feel hurt. I know what that feels like, because when I was young, a similar thing happened to me. Would you like to hear how I handled it?"

Be Supportive and Accept Your Child's Feelings

Be aware that being targeted for bullying may affect your child seriously and that talking about it may take a lot of courage. It is common for targets of bullying to experience anger, sadness, and fear, and it's essential that parents accept these feelings. Your child must know that whatever he is feeling is valid, even if his ways of handling the feelings or responding to the problem are inappropriate. With his own feelings accepted, your child feels encouraged to talk about the bullying and to look at different ways to handle it. Just the opposite happens when feelings are considered unimportant or an obstacle to a solution. When parents cut off a child and tell him not to feel what he is feeling, they are directly telling him not to trust his own experience. Feelings exist whether or not they're expressed, and unexpressed, or stuffed, feelings account for much of childhood depression. Girls are often admonished not to be angry, and boys are often taught that "big boys don't cry." These messages aren't helpful and can be damaging to children.

Make it clear to your child that you're taking what she is saying seriously, and that you will not minimize her feelings or the significance of the bullying. Don't laugh or make light of what your child is saying, no matter how trivial it may seem to you. And if hearing about the bullying upsets you, make sure you don't get caught up in your own feelings and ignore your child's. You may feel so angry toward the instigator and protective of your child that you feel a need to come up with a solution, even though your child is capable of solving the problem.

When your child's feelings are acknowledged, she feels validated, and therefore competent to examine and deal with the problem. You may feel uncomfortable hearing your child express strong feelings, but the fact that your child is willing to express them is a sign of strength. When you hear your child say that she is angry, sad, or afraid, remember that these feelings are OK.

Anger Is OK

Expressing anger appropriately can help to mobilize your child to stand up for himself. Anger is like gasoline. You can pour a gallon of gas in a puddle and light it, and you have an explosion—loud, potentially damaging, but for all practical purposes, a total waste of energy. You can take that same gallon of gasoline, put it in your tank, and drive somewhere. Anger is always powerful, and understanding and properly expressing it can be wonderful for a child who is a target of bullying. Parents can model the appropriate attitude toward anger. Here is an example, showing first a nonaccepting and then an accepting response to anger:

Nonacceptance of anger

CARLOS: "I'd like to punch out Joey. He keeps calling me names."

FATHER: "Don't talk like that. If you don't have something nice to say, don't say it."

Acceptance of anger

CARLOS: "I'd like to punch out Joey. He keeps calling me names."

FATHER: "Carlos, I understand that you're angry, and that's OK. But let's talk about some other things you can do when you're angry."

Sadness Is OK

The expression of grief is a way of saying that something important has been lost. For targets of bullying, this may be self-respect or a sense of belonging. Before your child can begin to explore ways that he can recover the loss, he needs to fully experience it. As we say in therapy, "Grief is the healing feeling." Only when someone expresses sadness can he be free to find ways to resolve the loss. If your child is sad and needs to cry, allow him to do so. This is especially important for boys in our society, because they are too often taught that crying is not an appropriate thing for boys to do. Here is an example, showing first a nonaccepting and then an accepting response to sadness:

Nonacceptance of sadness

JULIE: "Nobody at school likes me."

MOTHER: "Oh, it can't be that bad. You're always exaggerating."

Acceptance of sadness

JULIE: "Nobody at school likes me."

MOTHER: "You sound sad. It must not feel very good to think no one likes you. Would you like to talk about it?"

Fear Is OK

It's appropriate to be afraid of someone who threatens you verbally or physically. We often give kids, boys in particular, the message that only sissies are afraid. Talking about fear does not mean that your child can't deal with the problem. When you accept fear, you'll help your child recognize that this feeling is normal. That realization will provide her with the confidence to assertively confront the problem. You may want to tell about a time when someone hurt and frightened you, and how it turned out all right when you decided to deal with things directly. Here is an example, showing first a non-accepting and then an accepting response to fear:

Nonacceptance of fear	*Acceptance of fear*
NICK: "I'm afraid to go to school. I don't want to get beat up again."	NICK: "I'm afraid to go to school. I don't want to get beat up again."
MOTHER: "There's no reason to be afraid. Just ignore them and they won't bother you."	MOTHER: "I can understand why you are afraid. No one wants to get beat up. Would you like to talk about some ways to deal with those boys so you'd feel safer going to school?"

Really Listen

When your child tells you about peer abuse, you should practice *reflective listening* so that your child feels truly understood. This type of listening, also called *active listening*, involves listening carefully and nonjudgmentally for what the child is feeling, and then reflecting it back to the child. Give your child your full attention by stopping whatever else you may be doing. If you are unable to give your child your full attention at that moment, tell your child that you will talk with him as soon as you can. Make sure telephone calls or noise from the television or radio doesn't distract you from talking with your child, and make eye contact. Get as many details as you can, so you have the full picture of your child's situation.

In the example below, a mother talks with her daughter:

Nonactive listening

SUSIE: "Megan's so mean. She called me a tub of lard and wouldn't let me play dodgeball. All the other girls laughed at me."

MOTHER: "You know how Megan is. Just ignore her. How many times do we have to talk about this?"

Active listening

SUSIE: "Megan's so mean. She called me a tub of lard and wouldn't let me play dodgeball. All the other girls laughed at me."

MOTHER: "You must really feel left out. It hurts to be called names like that, and then for the other kids to laugh about it, too. Would you like to talk about it some more?"

Notice that with nonactive listening, Susie's feelings and experience are discounted. Minimizing a child's emotions or perceptions makes the child feel as if what she is really experiencing doesn't matter. The child feels rejected again, which is the last thing a child needs after being rejected by peers. In addition, Susie's mother is trying to solve her daughter's problem for her by offering immediate solutions.

It is understandable that parents often want to jump in and solve the problem, but what your child needs to know is that you hear her, that you understand her feelings, and that her feelings are justified. This gives her the implicit message that she is *normal*—that she isn't the problem—no matter what anyone else says or does, and she is capable of discovering effective ways to deal with the bullying.

Help Your Child Determine Possible Solutions

You need to remember that the bullying is your child's problem, not yours. You can give your child unconditional love, guidance, and your confidence in his or her ability, but your child is going to do the work required to stop the bullying. Don't criticize the way he's handled the problem so far. It's important for your child to know that you are there for him and ready to help in any way you can.

Help your child come up with ways to deal with the problem. A good way to generate ideas is to have a brainstorming session during which you and your child think of as many ideas as possible. When he comes up with an idea to deal with the bullying, congratulate him for his resourcefulness. Write each of them down, no matter how inappropriate they may be. Some may be silly, or even dangerous, but by listing all the options that come to mind, your child will have a sense of control over the actions he finally chooses. This is important for two reasons. First, he is more likely to buy into and try his own suggestions. Second, if you simply provided all the possible options, your child would not learn to trust his own judgments. You won't always be there to provide suggestions, and your child needs to learn how to think independently.

The following ideas are often helpful for a child to try when confronting bullying. If your child doesn't suggest them in your brainstorming session, you may want to slip in a few of them and ask your child to explain to you how he or she could use them.

- Talk to someone else nearby as if the bullying child isn't even there.

- Try not to be alone in potentially dangerous places, such as locker rooms, restrooms, or empty classrooms. Stay with a group, even if they're not friends.

- If a child demands that you hand over money or possessions, give what is requested, and then report it. The most important thing is to stay safe.

- Agree with the bullying child. Say, "You're right," and then walk away.

- Avoid the bullying child if necessary. Take a different route home or avoid places where the other child hangs out.
- Give yourself a pep talk. For example, tell yourself, "I know those things you're saying about me aren't true. I like who I am."
- Remember that fighting isn't an option. Children who bully tend to pick unfair fights, and you're likely to get hurt.
- Ask an adult for help if you're in physical danger.
- Remember that children who bully like to get a reaction. If you can learn to act as if it doesn't bother you, the bullying is likely to stop.

Analyze each option with your child. Help your child rule out those that may make the problem worse, put her in danger, or provoke violence. Make sure your child understands why you consider certain ideas unacceptable, and then focus on the ideas that are helpful and positive. A child often comes up with partial solutions. One child wrote, "Act real friendly and then if he acts friendly back, call him a mean name." In a case like this, focus on the positive aspect—acting friendly, which can be effective with some bullying children—and then discuss why name-calling might feel good for a moment, but would probably create even more problems and could even be dangerous.

Helping your child may involve talking with the school or other authorities. Be sensitive to the degree to which your child wants you to become actively involved. Children sometimes believe parental involvement will make the bullying worse. If the bullying doesn't involve serious physical or emotional harm or threats of serious physical harm, it is often appropriate to respect your child's wishes not to become actively involved. However, if serious threats are made or serious physical or emotional harm is being done, intervention is often necessary.

Helping Provocative Targets of Bullying

If you suspect your child may be a provocative target, it's important to understand how your child sees the problem, so you'll know what action to take. First, help your child identify the behaviors that cause the bullying child to react. Is your child hitting? Calling names? Following the other child around or getting into his or her personal space? Taking things off the child's desk?

Next, ask your child these questions: "Why do you behave this way? How do you want Jesse to react to the way you act?" Explain that we do everything for a reason, and sometimes we do things that get us in trouble because we don't think through all the alternatives. Your child may be unaware of his motivations, so you may need to present a variety of possible reasons and see whether your child can relate to any of them. Give your child plenty of time to think about your ideas. The following list, which provides some common motivations for provocative behavior, can help guide your discussion.

The child may be looking for ...

Attention seeker	Stimulation seeker	Revenge seeker
A way to make friends	A way to find excitement	A way to make the bullying child mad
. . .	. . .	. . .
A way to be cool or popular	A way to have fun	A way to get even (with either the instigator, bystanders, or adults who haven't taken action)

Helping the Attention Seeker

Children who crave attention to such a degree that they will risk the abuse of a bullying child suffer from low self-esteem. They have not learned to get their needs for recognition met in appropriate ways, and have learned that they can get loads of attention by provoking a bully.

Attention seekers may also identify inappropriately with a child who bullies. If a target feels weak and powerless, being involved with an aggressive child—even if only on the receiving end of abuse—can help the target feel more powerful, at least temporarily, though this is ultimately a self-defeating behavior. By engaging the bullying child in a game of cat-and-mouse, the target identifies with the bullying child and feels a part of the other child's world.

The attention-seeking child needs to learn how to feel good about herself and to feel strong in socially appropriate and healthy ways. Help your child discover and build upon hidden strengths and interests so she can feel good about herself without having to demand attention from others. The information in chapter 7 on building healthy self-esteem and making friends will be especially helpful for your child.

Helping the Stimulation Seeker

Stimulation seekers act impulsively without apparent regard for consequences. They have poor anticipatory skills and need to be taught how to foresee the likely consequences of their behavior and to make intelligent choices prior to action. Ask your child about ways he can find excitement or fun that are productive and don't bring on consequences like agitating a potentially bullying child. To help your child begin to predict the possible consequences of behavior, you can role-play, trading off roles of bullying child and target. Ask "What would happen if . . . ?" Since one of the most common underlying problems for stimulation seekers is attention-deficit/

hyperactivity disorder, it's also important to have a trained mental health professional evaluate whether AD/HD may contribute to your child's provocative behavior.

Helping the Revenge Seeker

The revenge seeker often feels alienated, misunderstood, and angry that the people who should be helping or intervening—peers and adults, including teachers, other school personnel, and perhaps parents—aren't. The desire for revenge may begin to encompass not only the bullying children, but also those people whom the target blames for not caring or helping. The revenge-seeking child may spin off into violent fantasies that involve serious harm.

It can be helpful to openly discuss the target's feelings. Sometimes all an angry provocative target needs is to be genuinely heard and then helped in taking steps to stop any bullying that is occurring. If that's the case, actively using the skill-building information in the following chapters will probably remedy your child's situation. However, revenge seekers are often seriously depressed or may suffer from other emotional problems that cloud the target's reasoning abilities, and such children require psychiatric treatment. If your child talks about seriously harming someone else, contact a mental health professional immediately.

Now that you've learned how to help your child explore her feelings and have gained an understanding of her perceptions of the problem, as well as what may be behind her responses to the bullying, and have brainstormed new approaches for your child to use to deal with the bullying, you're ready to help her take the next step in actively confronting bullying problems. The next chapter will help you teach your child how to communicate assertively with children who bully.

6

Teaching Your Child to Safely Stand Up to Bullying

Stand up for yourself! Don't let someone push you around! Hit him back! Give her some of her own medicine! Walk away! Ignore her! With so many conflicting cultural messages, it's no wonder parents and children are confused when confronted with bullying. Research on peer abuse consistently indicates how important it is for a target to respond assertively. Assertiveness goes a long way in protecting your child from bullying. But too often, we confuse "being assertive" with acting hostile toward another person, either verbally or even physically. So we'll explore what assertive behavior looks like and how you can teach your child this skill.

What Is Assertiveness?

Acting assertively simply means telling someone exactly what you want—directly, respectfully, and honestly. Most children, especially younger ones, have a limited repertoire of responses when it comes to dealing with peer conflict. They usually do one of two things: fight or withdraw. Learning to stand up for oneself assertively is important for all children because it gives them the ability to resolve a problem without having it escalate into a fight or end in shame. Learning how to be assertive is necessary for *all* relationships and will help your child to develop meaningful friendships as well as to prevent bullying. The quickest route toward healthy self-esteem is to mean what you say, and say what you mean.

Teaching assertiveness means helping your child learn to respond intelligently to provocations rather than letting someone push his buttons. It's normal for a child to feel angry when someone is threatening him, but it is not helpful to react aggressively. Matching someone insult for insult or choosing to fight will often lead to a more serious situation. Likewise, it is not helpful to retreat passively. When a child routinely retreats from confrontation, his fear intensifies, making it even more likely that the child will withdraw again the next time. It's especially important for children who tend to react either passively or aggressively to learn assertiveness skills, because an assertive child can effectively deal with many bullying scenarios on his own.

Let's look at a bullying situation that Eric encounters. In the first scenario he reacts passively and in the second aggressively.

Passive Response

Eric is a quiet, studious sixth-grader who usually sits with his friends at lunch. Today, the only place for him to sit is with some seventh-grade boys who are known to harass other kids. As soon as Eric starts eating, one of the boys across the table makes crude slurping sounds, and Eric looks up at him. The boy says, "What are you looking at, faggot?" and laughs with his friends. Eric, who feels humiliated and angry, looks down at his plate. He feels worse as they continue to bully him verbally, and he keeps trying to ignore them.

Aggressive Response

When Eric sits down and the boy sitting across the table says, "What are you looking at, faggot?" Eric picks up his lunch tray and throws it at the boy, hitting him in the face. The boy who made the insulting comment gets up, runs around the table, grabs Eric by the shoulders, pulls him onto the floor, and starts punching him.

■ ■ ■

In the first scenario, Eric saw no way to make the abuse stop, and he tried to withdraw from the situation. Like most children who respond passively, Eric felt vulnerable, overwhelmed, fearful, and ashamed. The more times he responds passively, the harder it is for him to believe in himself and in his abilities to deal effectively with conflict. When he responds aggressively, he takes the risk of getting physically hurt.

Anyone, like Eric, who's ever faced bullying knows it can be daunting, but assertively confronting a person who bullies is the most likely way to ensure that it won't happen again. Targets of bullying need to know they can stand up for themselves without putting themselves at risk of getting hurt.

Teaching Your Child Assertiveness

Assertiveness is a skill that can be learned and practiced at home, so your child will know what to do when a situation requires that she stand up to a child who bullies. Your child should also know when standing up to a bullying child is not a good idea. Sometimes it's smarter to choose other options. Learning assertiveness takes time, and you need to begin with whatever level your child is at.

Some children cry when they are confronted with bullying behavior. This response is certainly normal. It's scary to deal with an aggressive person. But when some children who bully see a child cry or act afraid, it can be like waving a red flag in front of a bull. It is helpful for a child to practice acting unfazed when confronted. This is not so difficult when you help your child understand that the emphasis is on *acting*. A child can act confident while still feeling scared inside. One benefit of acting confidently is that it often leads to real feelings of confidence. Assertive and confident body language can even help a child avoid becoming a target of bullying behavior.

Confident Body Language

Kids can learn to feel and look more confident by observing some simple rules about posture, walking, and eye contact.

Posture

Targets often stand or sit as if they are trying to make themselves invisible, as if they're saying, "Please don't notice me, I'll just hide here until you go away." One way targets do this is to slouch, making them look weak. Of course, this behavior is as ineffective as an ostrich sticking its head in the sand while the rest of its body is in clear sight.

What to do: Have your child practice standing up straight and tall with shoulders squared. This will give both your child and any would-be instigators of bullying the impression of confidence and the sense that your child has a right to be there.

Walking

Targets tend to walk either very quickly or very hesitantly. Both of these ways of walking give the impression of uncertainty and fearfulness.

What to do: Teach your child to walk tall with an easy stride. Practice walking with your child at a confident, relaxed pace.

Eye Contact

Targets, especially when they're shy, tend to make very little eye contact with people they don't know or with whom they feel uncomfortable. They may look at the floor as they walk and deliberately avoid looking at people when they are talking. This is another way these children attempt to make themselves invisible to potential instigators of bullying, but instead of protecting themselves, they've marked themselves as targets by appearing weak and fearful.

What to do: Have your child practice holding her gaze at eye level as she walks. Keeping the gaze up helps the child feel more comfortable and relaxed because she is more aware of what's going on around her. When she passes others, have her practice looking at them once in a while in a relaxed way, as if they were friends. Shy children can practice looking at people and smiling when they talk to them. It's important to help your child distinguish between appropriate eye contact and staring, because staring can be interpreted as confrontational, especially by children who bully.

Building Blocks to Assertiveness

In addition to looking confident, your child will need to know the four building blocks to assertiveness.

1. *Be direct, respectful, and honest.* Though it is normal to feel angry when bullied, striking out physically or with words only aggravates the problem, and passive acceptance of bullying behavior won't resolve the situation, either. Being assertive means being direct, respectful, and honest. On a behavior continuum, assertiveness falls midway between aggression and passivity.

Passive ——————— Assertive ——————— Aggressive

The example below will give you a good idea of the responses of children who fall at the ends and at the midpoint of this continuum. The children are responding to a child who has taken a ball from them.

Passive: "You can keep the ball. I'll play somewhere else."
Assertive: "Please give back the ball."
Aggressive: "Give me the damn ball back!"

As you can see, assertiveness is a clear and respectful expression of needs that allows a child to hold on to self-respect without being confrontational or being a doormat.

Children are usually so caught up in their anger when dealing with an aggressive person that they are very likely to want to yell at them, blame them, criticize them, negate them, and dehumanize them. The desire to attack is natural, but attacks don't solve anything. They just make things worse.

Teach your child the importance of treating the other child with respect, which admittedly is difficult. When a target refuses to give in to the natural urge to return disrespect, the bullying child is more likely to listen. Teach your child not to name-call, not to provoke a fight, and not to figure out some clever way to be mean or cruel to the other child as payback.

2. *Keep a safe physical distance.* No one likes to have his or her personal space invaded. An intrusion feels threatening and makes some children who bully even more angry. Instruct your child to stand back about four or five feet when practicing assertiveness. This amount of distance will prevent the other child from feeling challenged and will keep your child safe in case the bullying child decides to lash out physically.

3. *Don't make any physical contact.* Children can quickly move from being assertive to hitting, shoving, and pushing.

Being assertive means *no* physical contact. Giving in to an urge to fight can put your child in a dangerous situation.

4. *Use "I-messages."* When kids are angry with one another, "you-messages" start flying: "You're a punk." "You're a jerk." "You're a wuss." "You stink." "You're fat." "You're a loser." You-messages are blaming, shaming messages, and they make arguments escalate. An I-message, on the other hand, is direct, respectful, honest, and nonprovocative communication. To send an I-message, a child simply states his feelings and needs. Behind the actual words of an I-message, a target is saying that he doesn't deserve to be treated unfairly and refuses to accept the bullying child's negative opinion. Have your child practice using I-messages instead of you-messages.

You can teach him this template of an effective I-message: **"I don't like what you're saying (or doing), and I want you to stop."** It's best for your child to be specific about what's bothering him, so the instigator understands. For instance, "I don't like you calling me fat, and I want you to stop," or "I don't like it when you laugh at my clothes, and I want you to stop," or "I don't like it when you make fun of my family, and I want you to stop."

Many adults have learned to send I-messages in which they clearly state their feelings (sad, angry, hurt) in response to exactly what the other person has done. I don't find the inclusion of feelings necessary for children—especially younger children—when making I-statements, for several reasons. First, it can be very difficult for a child to be aware of exactly what he is feeling in the middle of a situation of peer abuse. Second, telling a bullying child how something impacts the target emotionally may just add fuel to the fire. The instigator may like to hear that the taunts are getting the desired results. As long as a child states directly, respectfully, and honestly that she doesn't like what the bullying child is doing and wants the abuse to stop, the I-message will be effective.

Let's return to Eric's experience in the cafeteria. Instead of shrinking away from his tormentors or escalating the situation with an aggressive response, Eric might say, "I don't like what you're saying, and I want you to stop." If the boys continue to hassle him, he can get up and leave. It's not cowardly to leave after he's asked them to stop; it's smart. He no longer feels shamed because he's said what he needs to say. If they don't listen, that's their problem, not his.

When to Stand Up to a Child Who Bullies

Children who bully like to harass isolated targets, but they are more likely to behave this way when they are with others, especially other bullying children. If your child can talk with the bullying child when that child doesn't have an audience of peers who encourage the abuse, the child is more likely to listen empathically to your child. Never encourage your child to talk with a bullying child privately if he doesn't feel safe or if the bullying child has a history of being physically abusive. Otherwise, the best time for your child to be assertive with a bullying child is at a time when no bullying is occurring and when he is in view of supportive people, preferably friends.

In the following example, Michael has strategically chosen the time and place to stand up to John. Notice how he incorporates confident body language and the building blocks to assertiveness.

> MICHAEL: (in the hallway after school with a teacher in sight, as well as a couple of Michael's friends who stand at a locker about twenty feet away) "John, I'd like to talk with you for a minute."

JOHN: "Yeah, what?"

MICHAEL: (speaking firmly while making eye contact and standing tall with squared shoulders at a distance about five feet from John) "I know you like cracking on me for being overweight, but I want you to stop."

JOHN: (speaking with a cocky swagger) "Hey, I only say it in fun."

MICHAEL: (continuing to practice confident body language) "Well, maybe so, but it's not funny to me. I bet you wouldn't want someone making fun of you."

This scene could go in several directions. John could simply ignore Michael's request, or even start bullying him then and there, or he may respect Michael's courage and tell him he's sorry and promise to stop the bullying. Whatever the outcome, Michael has made a big step toward overcoming shame by standing up to John. With his self-esteem more intact from this experience, Michael will probably assert himself more effectively in a future encounter with John if the bullying continues.

There are times when it's not safe to be assertive with a child who bullies. Help your child learn to recognize circumstances when being assertive is not the smart choice to avoid getting hurt or making the situation worse. A child should not confront a bullying child in the following situations:

- When threatened with physical violence
- When faced with a group of instigators
- When he or she doesn't feel safe

In these situations, it is most helpful for a child to try one of the following strategies:

Get adult help. Often adult help is the best solution. A child should inform a teacher or other adult in authority when he needs help.

Use distraction. Sometimes it is possible for a target to escape a threatening situation by getting an instigator's mind on something else. A child may say, "Hey, we're late for class," or "Here comes somebody." A targeted child may want to contrive a story to make the bullying child believe she is at risk of getting caught. For example, "I saw Mr. Jones heading this way just a minute ago."

Get away from the situation. A child should walk or run away from a threatening situation as quickly as possible and then look for help. If your child can't get away and is in serious danger of physical harm, instruct him to yell "Fire," the call for help that is most likely to elicit help from passersby.

Rehearsing Assertiveness

Assertiveness is a skill that improves with practice. Have your child rehearse confident body language and the building blocks to assertiveness so she feels prepared to use them when the pressure is on. Ask your child exactly what the bullying child has said, and help your child construct some I-messages to use the next time a bullying situation comes up. It's hard for children to remember to send an I-message while being harassed by another child, but I-messages will become second nature to your child with some practice at home. Have your child decide how he would like to respond the next time a confrontation occurs, and rehearse that response in role plays. You and your child can alternate playing the parts of the target and the instigator and can coach one another on what to do.

Unfortunately, assertiveness will not always stop a child who bullies. Sometimes a child will need to avoid the bullying child, use distraction, or ask an adult for help. Assertiveness does prevent the targeted child from accepting the negative judgment of the bullying child, so it *will* help to prevent your child from developing a sense of shame. This attitude paves the way for your child to develop healthy self-esteem and to learn friendship-making skills—two critical protectors against bullying.

7

Overcoming Problems Common to Targets of Bullying

"I hate my red hair!" "Why do I have to be the only Chinese kid in school?" "I wish I wasn't so smart." "I can't stand going to school. I don't have any friends." These complaints are typical of chronic targets of bullying, who tend to have greater than average problems with two issues of critical importance in any child's life: feeling good about themselves, and making and keeping friends. Once your child has learned the basics of assertiveness, you can then help her further overcome the negative impact of peer abuse with exercises to develop a healthy sense of self-esteem and to learn friendship-making skills.

Developing Healthy Self-Esteem

Every child, regardless of physical, intellectual, or emotional limitations, has the right to know that he is accepted, lovable, and profoundly valued. When parents, other adults, and peers send messages that a child belongs, the child will most likely develop a healthy sense of self-esteem. Children with healthy self-esteem easily accept themselves as they are. They don't compare themselves with others, wish they were different, or wish they were someone else. They understand that no one is perfect and that their most genuine and authentic self is the best person they can be.

A child with low self-esteem doesn't feel this same confidence. Children who are subjected to persistent peer abuse sometimes develop crippling self-doubt and fear of criticism. Self-doubt in such children becomes pervasive. They feel inadequate on a deep level, not simply because something is supposedly wrong with their anatomy, or their race, or their family background—the "faults" that may be highlighted in the taunts of the child who bullies. They feel ashamed of *who they are.* If a child is criticized for something she can help—for example, receiving an F on a test because she didn't study, she realizes that this was indeed a failing and maybe she deserved it. She can incorporate this learning and use it the next time a test comes along, improving her performance and feeling better about herself. But if she is criticized relentlessly for something out of her control—like facial features or height, her socioeconomic background, or a disability—she may begin to feel as if there is something wrong with *who she is.*

Though peer abuse can have a negative influence on a child's self-esteem, fortunately parents can do a great deal to help overcome these influences. Here are some ways you can help improve your child's self-esteem.

Teach a Positive Attitude
Don't let your child get away with putting himself down.

The neighborhood boys have picked on Ben for his lack of skill at batting. He strikes out almost every time he goes up to the plate, and no one wants to have him on their team. One day he comes home and says, "I've had it. I'm just a crummy ballplayer and I'm not going to play anymore." Ben's father, who knows that his son can throw well, is aware that a couple of the boys at the neighborhood baseball diamond continually razz Ben because of his weak hitting skills. Lately Ben has been focusing on what he can't do well, rather than on his strengths.

"You know, Ben," his father says, "I don't think you're a crummy ballplayer at all. You're a good fielder. Maybe if you spent some time at the batting cage, you could get to be just as good at hitting. Everybody is naturally good at some things, while other things come harder. I'm sure that with practice, you can learn to hit really well, too. How about we go down to the batting cage this evening and hit some balls?"

Most clouds really do have silver linings, and it's often the job of a parent to help the child find them.

Give Specific and Generous Praise
Notice your child's accomplishments and praise her for having met a difficult challenge.

Targets of bullying often feel discouraged and don't recognize their accomplishments. We all appreciate pats on the back and like to know that our efforts are recognized. However, a child doesn't develop healthy self-esteem simply from our praising every little effort made. Rather, we help our child develop self-esteem when we help her to recognize that she has met a specific challenge and has grown in some way. Sometimes taking on a difficult challenge, even if it doesn't result with particular success, is success enough. Much of what accounts for success in life—whether social, intellectual, or material—entails skill-building and practice. Instead of praising with broad, general statements, praise your child for specific accomplishments and behaviors, especially challenges that you know were difficult for her. The following examples will help you distinguish between specific praise that helps build healthy self-esteem, and general praise, which is less effective.

Specific Praise	*General Praise*
"Good work on your math test. I know you really studied hard for it."	"You're a good student."
"I was really proud of you at the play today. You ad libbed so well when you forgot your lines that I don't think anyone noticed!"	"Good job today."

Be a Gloom Buster

Teach your child to think optimistically.

Many people expect the worst from life; you can spot them a mile away. We call these people pessimists. Sometimes children with low self-esteem are pessimistic because they feel discouraged, yet a pessimistic attitude pushes away other children. If your child has a pessimistic attitude, he or she will have trouble making and keeping friends. Teaching children to think optimistically doesn't mean they need to believe that every day is sunshine and that roses don't have thorns, rather that they can be thankful for the rain and that thornbushes have roses. Optimism means to be realistic, as well as to be hopeful and to look on the bright side.

A child is usually pessimistic for these reasons:

- The child is exaggerating the truth to get someone to pay attention.
- The child is trying to avoid facing something difficult.
- The child is trying to elicit sympathy.

Follow these three steps to help your child change the way he approaches life when seeing only gloom:

- Practice active listening, paying attention to what your child seems to be feeling and reflecting those feelings.
- Notice your child's use of pessimistic language, particularly absolute words like *can't, always, never, nobody,* and *everyone.*
- Help your child change the way he looks at a situation by restating it in more optimistic terms.

The examples below will help you understand your role as a gloom buster.

Your child says:	You say:
"Nobody ever wants to play with me."	"It sounds like you're feeling lonely and you'd like to have more friends, but what about your friend Lisa who was just over yesterday?"
"I *can't* do this math."	"Sounds like you're really frustrated, but new things take time to learn. I'm sure if you're patient, you'll get it. Have you tried using the formula you learned last week?"

Use Humor
Show your child how to take life a little more lightly.

Chronic bullying tends to leave a child feeling sensitive, so targets of bullying have a hard time laughing at themselves. Their nerves are raw, and they feel the need to be constantly on the defensive. If a child can learn to laugh at herself, however, children who bully aren't going to have much power. One of the best ways targets can respond to children who bully is to find humor in what they say. Help your child think of some silly, nonprovocative one-liners to toss at a child who bullies in order to defuse a situation.

Model healthy self-esteem by not taking yourself too seriously. Let your child see you laughing at yourself when it's appropriate. Your child needs to understand that true teasing doesn't mean others don't like them—in fact, good-hearted teasing often means just the opposite. It can help for a child to learn to laugh and even tease back with a joke that's also in fun. Your child can learn from your lead how to take life a little more lightly.

Encourage Your Child to Take Reasonable Risks
Teach your child the value of having the courage to make mistakes.

A child who says, "I've never done that before, and I think I can," shows a healthy sense of self-esteem. But children who are afraid to take risks will always struggle with their self-esteem. Experiencing the sense of genuine accomplishment that comes with trying new things, meeting new people, and taking on difficult challenges is a big part of self-esteem. Giving in to the fear of trying new things or meeting challenges is a great impediment to personal growth, while the opposite—facing fears directly and doing what needs to be done *despite* the fear—is the surest way for a child to build confidence.

Children whom peers have repeatedly abused often feel as if they must do things perfectly, or not at all. This leads to procrastination and performance anxiety. Targets of bullying are often afraid to try new things, especially in the presence of peers, due to fear of ridicule if they make mistakes.

Encourage literally means "to give courage" to another person, and parents have the power to pass on courage to their children. You can help your child by sharing any challenges you have faced despite your fears. Encourage your child to take reasonable risks instead of taking the easy road. This may take the form of embracing athletics or challenging extracurricular activities in music, art, or drama; spending more time with other children in social activities, such as Scouts or 4-H or youth camp, if your child tends to be shy or withdrawn; or asserting himself with a child who bullies. The new kid may or may not want to be your child's friend. Maybe your child will fall on his face or forget his lines at the spring play. Maybe she'll be the worst basketball player her school's ever seen. But maybe not. Children with healthy self-esteem don't let these risk factors stop them.

A healthy sense of self-esteem is the most important quality a child can possess. Parents don't help develop self-esteem in their children simply by offering affirmations, gushing praise, or making them wear "I'm special" buttons. Self-esteem doesn't come that easily. Building self-esteem is a gradual process. It's critical that your child sees you model healthy self-esteem on a daily basis. But probably more important is that your words and actions consistently demonstrate that you really, truly believe in your child.

Helping Your Child Make Friends

Children with good friendships have very little trouble with bullying, since children who bully tend to seek out as targets those who are socially isolated. Perhaps more than anything else, making good friends can help your child avoid bullying. In many cases, socially isolated children are temperamentally shy and are selected as targets because they have no one to defend them. These children need to put extra effort into learning the necessary social skills for making friends. Let's take a look at some ideas that can help a child who has difficulty making friends.

Making Friends Takes Time and Effort

Jessica, a shy child who wishes she had more friends, is a favorite of her teachers. She spends most of her lunchtime alone and talks with the teachers at recess while the other children are playing. Jessica gets verbally bullied for being a nerd because she seems to like her teachers better than her peers. After school, instead of inviting over another girl, she spends all the time that she's not studying in front of the television. She chooses the safety of adults or the electronic anesthesia of television over the risk of making friends with children whom she perceives as socially superior. Jessica's fear of social inferiority would gradually disappear if she would work on friendship-making skills and begin to see success.

With friendship, as with anything else in life, you get what you put into it. Some children, particularly those who are shy or depressed, don't put enough effort into finding, making, and keeping friends. They think it should be easier than it is. A child like Jessica needs to know that friendships take time and effort, and that not all of their efforts at making friends will work. For a shy child, making friends means leaving the comfort zone of solitary activities like watching television, playing video games, or reading to the exclusion of being with peers. Excessive time spent in solitary activity robs children of valuable moments they could enjoy with peers.

Children who spend too much time alone should be encouraged to invite same-gender friends over to the house for one-to-one play time, which may or may not involve overnights. Though opposite-gender friendships can be very good for children, boys and girls who have difficulty making friends will become more comfortable with their gender roles by developing several close same-gender friends.

To Make a Friend, You Must Be a Friend

Children with few friends often create their own anxiety by constantly wishing things were different instead of taking the necessary action to change things. They often make the situation worse by avoiding the very activities and situations where potential friends are likely to be. When they do find themselves with other children on the playground or in the neighborhood, they spend all their emotional energy being afraid and waiting for someone to act friendly with them instead of extending themselves to others. Shy children especially tend to focus so much on their own anxiety and discomfort in being with others that friendship-building becomes a tremendous effort. Just as "all the world loves a lover," all the world loves a friend. *Acting* friendly leads to *feeling* friendly, which in turn leads to good friendships. If your child is shy, have him practice acting friendly, just as you had your child practice how to be assertive with children who bully. At home, he can practice asking others to play or can practice engaging in friendly conversation while making eye contact. Once your child feels comfortable, ask him to try out these behaviors at school.

Be a Good Sport

Sasha's mother watched Hannah storm out the front door with her favorite video game tucked under her arm.

"See if I ask you to play again," snapped Hannah.

"What happened?" asked Sasha's mother.

"Oh, she makes me sick," Sasha groaned. "All I said was, 'Ha-ha, I won again,' and she acts all hurt. What a baby."

Sometimes a child who has problems interacting with peers needs to learn how to be a gracious winner as well as a good loser. Being a sore loser or bragging about winning can alienate other children. A child's sportsmanship can often be traced to his or her parents. If your child is a bad sport—complaining about a raw deal from the umpire or blaming another child on the team for losing, or strutting around after a win and mocking the losing team—look to yourself. Are you gracious whether you win or lose? Do you model good sportsmanship when you're playing sports or games? When you're watching sports or game shows on TV? When you're watching your child compete? Our society is preoccupied with winning at all costs, instead of showing respect for good effort. Children need to learn that what's important is doing your best, not perfection.

Organized Activities

A shy second-grader with a wry smile, Randy is smaller than most of the boys in his class. Until recently he spent all of his free time in front of the TV, helping his mother, or playing Chutes and Ladders with his younger brother. At school, he spent playground time with girls, for which the boys ridiculed him and called him a baby. Randy, who doesn't act feminine and doesn't particularly like the games the girls play, really wanted the boys to accept him and to play rougher "boy's games." But Randy was already feeling typecast and didn't know how to break out of the role in which he found himself. By second grade, boys who hang around with girls are going to get harassed. Unless this choice feels satisfying and perfectly natural for a boy, he needs to learn how to socialize better with boys.

It concerned Randy's mother that he didn't invite boys to the house to play after school. When she asked him about this, she discovered what she had sensed—that Randy was having trouble making same-gender friends. She knew her son often watched *The Karate Kid,* a videotape in the family's collection. In hopes that karate classes would help Randy learn to make friends with other boys, she enrolled him in an introductory series of classes. She knew that the basis of martial arts training is restraint, respect for the other person, and development of self-confidence. Randy's response was lukewarm—more out of fear that he'd look silly or get picked on by boys in the karate class than from a lack of interest—but his mother had already enrolled him.

"Do I have to go?" Randy asked.

"Yes," she said. "I think it's important that you try it. I want you to go four times. If you decide you don't like it at that point, we can talk about how you feel."

At the first meeting, Randy made friends with a boy from another school who was a lot like him. His attitude dramatically improved and he showed more self-confidence in dealing with boys at school. After the second class, he was playing with the boys at recess and in a very short time went on to develop several close friendships with male classmates. After the fourth class, he told his mother his goal was an orange belt, and she no longer worried about his ability to make friends with boys at school.

One of the best ways for children to meet friends is through organized activities. Common interests are the lifeblood of developing friendships. Some children, like Randy, benefit from organized activities outside of school because they can escape the often-unhappy roles in which they are confined at school.

Sports leagues, Boy Scouts, Girl Scouts, Campfire Girls, 4-H, church clubs, Boy's and Girl's Clubs, drama clubs and youth theater, youth orchestras and other musical ensembles, and martial arts classes are just a few examples of activities that will help elementary- through middle-school-aged children develop their friendship-making skills.

But be careful not to overinvolve your child in activities. Children—especially before high school—shouldn't need day planners! Organized activities, while fun for a child and very beneficial for social, intellectual, artistic, and physical development, shouldn't fill all her free time. If the balance is tipped too far on the side of organized activities, your child's social skills may actually suffer. Without enough unstructured time to spend playing one-on-one, talking, and practicing problem solving with children of her choosing, your child won't develop meaningful friendships. Parents can be a great help in teaching children how to balance structured and unstructured time.

Learn to Do Things Other Children Enjoy

Christopher gets hassled every day at school by a group of other sixth-graders because he sings in the choir, plays the violin in the school orchestra, and shows no apparent interest in doing anything outside the narrow confines of music. Christopher is aware that he has become angrier and angrier over the years at kids who bully him because of his passion for music. He tells himself he's above them, and he refuses to lower himself to engage in any activities other boys his age enjoy, like sports or video games, even though these age-appropriate activities could be fun and might help him gain friends.

Sometimes children have a hard time making friends not simply because their interests are different from those of other children, but because they show no interest whatsoever in the activities of their peers. It's certainly important for children to pursue their individual interests, whether or not other children appreciate them. But it's also necessary for children to realize that they live in a community of peers, and part of being in a community is learning to value and appreciate at least some of the activities in which peers engage.

Try to broaden your child's range of interests. Encouraging a wide variety of activities will enable him to feel comfortable in different social environments and with a wider selection of peers.

Treat Other Children the Way You'd Like to Be Treated

Seth, a fourth-grader, complains to his parents almost daily that no one at school likes him. His father set up a conference with his son's teacher, who confirms that Seth is ostracized by other boys and usually spends playground time by himself on the monkey bars. She goes on to say that Seth often aggravates the situation by taunting other boys or grabbing the ball they're playing with and kicking it away from them.

Finding, making, and keeping friends means not only getting out with other children, playing games, and doing activities other children enjoy, but also *being* a good friend. Sometimes socially isolated children are attention seekers or stimulation seekers. They do things that aggravate other children, act inappropriately silly, or make demands that provoke other children to alienate or bully them. If you suspect your child is a provocative target of bullying, try to find out what he or she is doing to prevent friendships from developing. You'll probably need to talk with your child's teachers to understand how his or her peer relationships are playing out at school.

8

What If Nothing Works?

Suppose you've tried working with your child on assertiveness skills, friendship-making skills, and self-esteem, but she continues to be a target of bullying. At this point, it can be useful to consider additional options. Contacting the school to collaborate on a solution, seeking the help of a mental health professional, or even contacting the police are appropriate measures to take in many situations.

When to Contact the School

Melinda had been putting up with a seventh-grade classmate's bullying on the school bus for several weeks. The longer it went on, the more afraid she became. Zachary, a new boy at school, started out by asking her for a kiss. When she refused, he held her against the seat and kissed her. He told her that she was his girlfriend and he had better not see her talking to any other boys. Melinda replied firmly that she was not, and she would talk with whomever she wished. Melinda told the bus driver, who said she should change seats. For several days when he walked by her bus seat, Zachary called her profane names so quietly that no one else could hear. Each time she told him to stop. Melinda tried desperately to ignore Zachary, but he was persistent. One day she was talking with a boy, and Zachary whispered in her ear from the bus seat behind her, "I know where you live, and I'm coming over when your parents are gone."

Melinda's experience is a good example of when a parent needs to contact the school. Older children may fear that school involvement could make the problem worse and ask you not to involve school authorities. However, when a child's numerous attempts to deal with a child who bullies have met with no success and there's a threat of serious physical or emotional harm, it's necessary for parents to contact the school. The school has a legal responsibility to protect children while they are at school, at school-sponsored activities, and on the school bus. School personnel are obligated to provide a safe and peaceful environment that is conducive to learning. For this to happen, school officials must be aware of bullying situations. Schools can't help if parents don't tell them precisely what's happening.

How to Collaborate with the School

Though many schools are quick to deal with a bullying problem, some are not. Don't let the school minimize the problem; it's a problem if there is evidence of physical or emotional harm. Don't accept being brushed aside with noncommittal comments like "we'll take a look at it" or "we'll take care of it." Make it clear that you expect the school to provide a safe environment for your child. However, don't take an adversarial position with the school—don't lose your temper, swear, or shout.

Learn the school's behavior code. Most school systems have clear policies on what constitutes appropriate behavior and have disciplinary consequences for violations of the code. A school's behavior code should include a clear description of how the school deals with peer abuse. Sometimes bullying does more than break the school's behavior code—sometimes it's illegal. For example, Title IX of the 1972 Education Act and Title VII of the 1964 Civil Rights Act requires schools to protect students from sexual harassment.

The following steps will help you collaborate with your child's school:

1. *Get as Much Information as Possible about the Bullying from Your Child.* Children are often reluctant to give all the details, but get as many as you can. To get this information, ask your child specific questions:
   - Who is doing the bullying?
   - Is it one or more children who are bullying you?
   - Have any children witnessed the bullying?
   - Exactly what is being said or done?
   - Have you ever been hurt physically?
   - How often does the bullying happen?
   - Does it happen at the same time or the same place?
   - How do you feel about the bullying?

2. *Set Up a Meeting for You and Your Child with the Appropriate School Officials.* Before making calls, refer to the school policy manual and the behavior code to determine whom you should contact. This may include the principal, school counselor, and any teachers involved. Don't just call the school to report the problem. Bullying is important enough to merit a face-to-face meeting. At the meeting, tell school personnel the details about the bullying that your child has given you.

3. *Coordinate an Action Plan.* The goal of the meeting is to come up with a plan that will stop the bullying. Ask your child what he or she would like to see happen. Sometimes a child will have good suggestions. When teachers and school officials know that bullying is happening at a particular

place, at a particular time, they're in a better position to suggest what can be done. You, your child, and the school personnel should write up the plan and decide how it will be implemented. The action plan must include a serious talk with any child involved in the bullying and his or her parents. Many times the plan will also include that the school provide better supervision for your child, a step that usually stops or at least reduces the bullying. Make sure everyone has a copy of the plan and understands its purpose and specific measures to be taken. Before you and your child leave, schedule a follow-up meeting for approximately a week later to review how the action plan is working.

4. *Put the Plan into Action.* Implement the plan.

5. *Review the Plan with a Follow-up Meeting.* Ask your child whether the situation has improved. Work together with the school to adjust the plan to ensure your child's safety. The example below will give you an idea of how sometimes even a slight change can halt the bullying.

Sixth-grader Anthony complained to his father about two boys his age who called him "nerd" and "geek" and shoved him around when they found him alone. He'd tried to be assertive or ignore them, but neither tactic helped much. Anthony said the bullying was the worst at lunch because his last morning class met on the end of the school building opposite the cafeteria. By the time he'd arrive for lunch, the seats near his friends were taken. He felt secure with his friends and thought the bullying wouldn't occur if he could sit with them. His father asked the principal if Anthony could leave class two minutes early so he could be with his friends at lunch. The principal agreed to his request. In addition, the principal met with the two boys and their parents, informed them of the problem and the solution, and assigned after-school suspension. In the follow-up meeting the next week, Anthony, his father, and the principal celebrated the success of their action plan, which had stopped the bullying.

When to Contact a Therapist

It's natural for parents to be hopeful that their children's problems with peer abuse will diminish when their children work on improving assertiveness, self-esteem, and the skills for making friends. In many cases, they do. But certain indicators are serious enough to warrant getting help from a mental health professional. Targets of bullying may suffer from depression, excessive anxiety of school, or post-traumatic stress disorder. In deciding if your child needs therapy, the main criteria to consider are whether he or she seems to be improving on his or her own and whether the symptoms are serious enough to interfere with daily functioning.

Depression

You need to take any indication that your child is depressed seriously. Children who are chronically bullied stand a much greater chance of having suicidal thoughts than the average child who isn't bullied. If your child seems preoccupied with death or has mentioned or threatens suicide, it's critical that he or she be assessed immediately by a mental health professional. It's uncommon that a child will ask to see a counselor or therapist, so it's important that parents recognize these common signs of this treatable emotional disorder.

- Chooses to spend time in solitary activities (TV, video games) instead of with peers
- Threatens or attempts suicide
- Performs poorly at school
- Appears apathetic
- Displays unexplainable fatigue
- Sleeps too much or not enough

- Displays poor appetite or eats excessively
- Appears sad
- Has unpredictable outbursts of anger

Anxiety

Sometimes a child will become so fearful of attending school or associating with peers that excessive anxiety develops. When a fear becomes so persistent that everyday functioning is affected, a professional evaluation is recommended. Consider having a mental health professional talk with your child if he or she exhibits any of these behaviors:

- Has a persistent fear of attending school
- Cries, clings to you, "freezes up," or has tantrums when it's time to go to school
- Refuses to attend school
- Often gets sick at school and needs to come home, or has frequent headaches, stomachaches, or other physical symptoms when it's time for school or school-related activities

Post-traumatic Stress Disorder

Chronic targets of peer abuse can develop a serious condition called post-traumatic stress disorder. PTSD develops when abuse is serious, especially in response to physical or sexual assault. If your child has any of the following in relation to a traumatic event, consult a mental health professional:

- Nightmares
- Avoidance of situations or places that remind him or her of the traumatic event
- Frequent flashbacks (unwanted mental "reruns") of the traumatic event
- Hypervigilance, meaning that a child startles easily
- Uncharacteristic outbursts of anger and agitation

A thorough evaluation can help you decide if counseling may be helpful. Targets of bullying can benefit enormously from therapy with a social worker, a psychologist, a psychiatric nurse, or a psychiatrist. The best way to locate a good child/adolescent mental health professional in your community is by word of mouth. Ask around to find out who is well known and competent. Most child and adolescent mental health professionals also practice family therapy, seeing the whole family together. To help a child who has been a target of bullying, a mental health professional may use any of a number of strategies, including individual or family therapy, social skills training, or group therapy.

When to Contact Legal Authorities

Whether legal authorities should become involved in a bullying situation hinges on one central question: Has a delinquent act been committed? Different states and provinces have different laws, and addressing them individually is beyond the scope of this book. In most jurisdictions, however, the same laws that apply to adults for such crimes as battery, assault, stalking, intimidation, harassment, and disorderly conduct also apply to children. If you believe your child may have been the target of a crime, you should contact the police.

Although chapters 9, 10, and 11 are addressed specifically to parents of children who bully, as a parent of a targeted child you may find benefit in reading them. These chapters will give you an idea of the typical belief systems under which children who bully operate and the difficulties that parents of these children need to overcome to change their child's behavior pattern.

WHAT TO DO IF YOUR CHILD BULLIES

9

How to Know If
Your Child Bullies

Many parents have no doubt that their child is bullying others—
they receive reports about their child's behavior from school,
from other authorities, or from parents of other children. In
some cases, however, the aggressive behavior pattern isn't as
visible or doesn't get reported, so a parent needs to understand
the signs that a child needs help with a bullying problem. Your
child may have a problem with bullying if he or she

- Enjoys putting down other people
- Doesn't care whether others' feelings are hurt
- Shows disrespect for authority
- Shows a fascination with neo-Nazism or racial
  supremacy
- Shows disrespect for the opposite sex
- Makes jokes about rape or other violence against
  women
- Enjoys fighting
- Believes "everything should go my way"
- Won't admit mistakes

- Lies frequently to get out of trouble
- Thinks rules are stupid
- Deliberately hurts pets or other animals
- Believes other people aren't to be trusted
- Refuses to admit fear
- Uses anger to get what he or she wants
- Has an attitude of superiority over other children

If one or more of these items applies to your child, he or she may need your help to correct a self-defeating and potentially lifelong pattern of bullying behavior. The more that apply, the more serious the potential problem.

What Makes a Child More Likely to Bully?

Since bullying behavior can cause such serious problems for children who bully and for their targets, it's important to understand why some children bully, and some don't. Certain characteristics of children and their families are conducive to bullying behavior. The following quiz will help you test your knowledge of these common characteristics. Copy this list from the book and then circle **T** for the statements you think are true, and **F** for those you think are false on your copy.

Children are more likely to bully other children if:

T F They think having someone fear them is the same thing as having someone respect them.

T F They think walking away from a fight is for wimps.

T F They think they are better than others.

T F One or both of their parents have alcohol or drug problems.

T F Their parents are divorced or separated, and the parents do not get along well with their former partners.

T F There have been problems with domestic violence in the family.

T F Their parents are mistrustful of marriage or relationships in general.

T F Their parents don't trust each other.

T F One or both of their parents is involved in criminal activity.

T F When their parents are divorced, they continue to fight and argue, in such a way that the child feels like a "go-between."

T F Their parents argue a lot.

T F They are left alone for long periods of time without adult supervision.

T F They feel the adults around them don't care about them.

T F They are physically disciplined when they misbehave.

T F A parent punishes them more severely when in a bad mood.

T F One or both parents see physical fighting as an acceptable way to resolve problems.

T F One or both parents see put-downs or insults as an acceptable way to resolve problems.

T F One or both parents hold attitudes that others may find bigoted, racist, or sexist.

T F They are called names or put down by parents.

T F One or both parents exhibited bullying behaviors as children.

T F Their parents are extremely strict.

T F Their parents are extremely permissive.

For each item, a T answer indicates a situation conducive to bullying behavior in children. If many T answers apply to your family or to your child, you may have to consider that your child needs your help to modify his or her behavior. More important, you should think about what entrenched family behavior may contribute to your child's bullying behavior. Please remember—these are just guidelines. Some families function well and are happy, yet they still may have to help a child overcome a pattern of bullying behavior.

Common Issues in Families
of Children Who Bully

Children who bully come from families at all socioeconomic levels and across all racial and ethnic lines. Fortunately, the tendency to bully isn't built into the genes. If that were the case, we could just throw in the towel. But because our children aren't inherently programmed to bully, it's our responsibility to examine what's behind the behavior when we see it. Certain issues are common to families of children who bully, and it's helpful to understand that when parents address these situations, the child's behavior and attitude often change.

Parental Relationship Is Strained

Parents of children who bully tend to have strained relationships with their spouses or partners, and subsequently separation and divorce in these families are common. Providing consistent, effective parenting is difficult when partners aren't emotionally supportive of and cooperative with one another and grudges are held. In the following summary of Lisa's family, it's clear that the strain in her parents' marriage is triggering Lisa to seek some control by bullying an unassertive classmate.

Lisa's mother and father have considered divorce for several years. They argue frequently, and usually their arguments are unfair. They yell at one another in front of Lisa, flinging insults and rubbing in past mistakes. Her parents are so caught up in their own problems that they won't listen to Lisa when she asks them to stop fighting. In addition, sometimes Lisa's mother will confide in her daughter about the marital problems, speaking to Lisa as if she were an adult. Lisa feels helpless and angry. Lately, Lisa has taken out her anger on another seventh-grader, a quiet, studious girl. She enjoys the feeling of power and control she gets from calling the girl names.

Children need to know that home is a safe place, emotionally as well as physically. A child also needs to know she's not responsible for her parents, in the way Lisa's mother expects her to serve as counselor for her. No marriage is perfect, but parents need to work out their problems respectfully. So wrapped up in themselves, Lisa's parents don't have energy for her. The longer their marital problems continue, the angrier their daughter becomes. As long as Lisa's parents don't pay attention to her emotional needs, Lisa may continue to take out her anger at school.

Families do not need to be perfect or intact in order to prevent bullying behavior in their children, but parents need to be aware of and sensitive to the messages they pass on to their children.

Children Who Bully Need More Supervision

The less time children spend with adults, the more likely it is that they'll engage in peer abuse. Kids need the guidance, positive direction, and supervision that only adults can provide, and in families where parents are overworked, children don't get as much attention as they should. In families where parents are present but rarely interact with their children, the children don't get the nurturing and discipline they need. Ryan's aggressive behavior in the description below isn't unusual for kids who spend too much time without adult guidance.

Ryan's parents divorced when he was three, and he has not seen his father since then. Ryan's mother works two jobs to make ends meet, and she feels bad that she is not home often enough to provide adequate supervision. Ryan has older friends in the neighborhood who have been in trouble, and she worries that they are a bad influence.

Ryan used to cry himself to sleep because his father would promise to visit but wouldn't show up. At eleven, he says he doesn't care anymore, yet the deep anger toward his father comes out as physical and verbal bullying of peers at school. The tough exterior Ryan shows to the world belies the deep sadness he feels inside. Ryan's mother is doing the best she can, but the lack of adequate adult supervision coupled with Ryan's anger at having been abandoned by his father is a dangerous combination.

Children should spend most of their time under the close watch of caring adults. Parents, like Ryan's mother, who cannot afford to take time off from work to watch a child, should make sure the child is under the care of a responsible relative or enrolled in closely supervised activities.

Children Who Bully Often Receive Ineffective Discipline

Parents and caretakers of children who bully are more likely to use physical punishment than noncorporal methods of discipline. Children who bully are much more likely than their peers to be spanked, whipped, or even beaten when they misbehave.[1] This kind of physical discipline teaches children that physical aggression is the way to handle conflict.

Children who bully are also inconsistently disciplined. Sometimes it's hard for parents to keep emotions in check when dealing with a discipline problem. In families of children who bully, the children tend to get punished more severely when the parent is in a bad mood. What may be a small matter one day can be a huge ordeal the next, just because mom or dad is having a hard day. In the example below, the physical discipline Trevor's father believes will correct his son's behavior serves only to fuel Trevor's own use of physical violence.

Trevor is a fourth-grader whose father believes the most effective way to discipline his son is physical punishment. He thinks breaking Trevor's resistance to his authority will serve his son well in life. Typically, he will spank Trevor on the buttocks, but sometimes he tells Trevor to cut off a branch from a tree with which he'll whip Trevor. Trevor has been getting into fights at school since first grade, and he gets whipped at home whenever his father gets a bad report from school. However, the discipline doesn't seem to help, and the fights are getting more serious.

Despite the intentions of Trevor's father, physical discipline teaches Trevor only that aggression is the best way to deal with conflict. Trevor applies the lesson he learned at home while he's in school. Although Trevor's father feels that violence is the only way to discipline his son, learning about more sympathetic and effective disciplinary measures that would be easier on him and his son could remedy this frustrating situation. Trevor's bullying will probably continue until his father finds more nurturing, nonphysical ways to deal with his son's behavior.

Children Who Bully See and Hear More Violence

The more violence a child sees and hears, the more he or she becomes desensitized to it. In some families, bullying isn't considered such a big deal. Fighting and put-downs are seen as acceptable ways to manage conflict. In these families, children learn that insults are appropriate responses when they are challenged. Children are especially damaged when they watch their parents exchange insults, both apparently unfazed by the violence of their interaction.

The following are some examples of how families may condone violence:

- Calling children or other family members hurtful "pet names," like "dumbass," "wimp," or "fatso"
- Fighting, shoving, slapping, grabbing, or in any way touching someone in anger
- Using insulting or bigoted language toward anyone, such as "nigger" or "white trash"

- Criticizing a child's potential with comments such as "You'll never amount to anything," "You're just not that bright," or "You're a loser"

In families where abusive language is common, parents must work especially hard to pay attention to their words and to remember that their children are affected by everything they say. They must also learn to control their anger so they don't act out physically when they're upset.

Don't feel discouraged if some of the examples hit close to home—plenty of parents recognize parts of themselves in these scenarios. Remember that you are in the best position to help your child overcome problems with bullying. If you learn to recognize unhealthy patterns in the way your family communicates and disciplines, you will be able to spot the behaviors and attitudes that trigger bullying behavior. As a concerned and observant parent, you are well on the way to helping your child become the sensitive and caring adult he or she is meant to be.

10

Overcoming Problems Common to Children Who Bully

As a parent, you want your child to know how to act responsibly, deal honestly with others, work toward a peaceful resolution of problems that involve others, and understand and respect another person's feelings. Home is the best place for children to learn the values and attitudes behind these social skills, which aren't so much taught as they are "caught" when children observe them in practice in their parents' behavior. Children look to their parents as role models for appropriate behavior and attitudes. Parents *must* demonstrate these skills in daily life. The informal lessons your child catches are worth hours of lectures. You are the most important teacher your child will ever have, and what you do says volumes more than what you say.

When a child is aggressive toward other children, parents must assume a vital role to help change not only the child's immediate behavior, but also the course of her life. You may be frustrated because you have *already* been working hard to improve things—but nothing seems to change and you feel like you're spinning your wheels. It may be useful to think about what you'd do if your car were stuck in a rut. Most likely you'd remain wedged tight after flooring the accelerator a few times. So you'd get out of the car, assess the situation, find something to place under the wheels to give you a boost out, and then happily drive on. Likewise in child rearing: It may be that some of your role modeling isn't appropriate, but once you determine the negative messages your behavior is sending, you can acquire skills and begin to change your behavior. This chapter will help you assess behavior that's keeping your wheels spinning and working against your goal of helping your child to reach her fullest potential. It also provides ideas to help you become a more effective role model and offers advice for interrupting bullying behavior in your child. When you put these new skills to work, you'll find that your family life is happier and that the challenges of parenting become far more rewarding and enjoyable.

As you learn more positive ways to interact with your child, let her know about the ways you intend to improve your relationship together, the ways you plan to change your behavior, and how you hope your entire family will benefit from these changes. Let your child know that you're all in this together, and have family conversations about how to improve the ways you act and speak to one another.

Teaching Your Child to Care about Others

Empathy means putting ourselves in another's place and being able to appreciate and understand how that person must feel. It is an attitude of the heart that comes from genuinely caring about someone else and believing that another person is just as important as we are. When we try to see the world through the eyes of another person, our vision clears and we become more humane. We realize how important it is to celebrate each other's joys and to help bear one another's sufferings. We understand that it feels good to care about someone else. Children who are empathic have better friendships, get into less trouble, and are more respected by their peers and adults.

Empathy is a natural response for most children. In a nursery, when one baby starts crying, other babies start crying. We can observe it when we watch two small children playing. When one child starts crying, the other child goes over to ask if she's all right. As children mature, developmental psychologists tell us, they become more and more capable of putting themselves into another's place. By later childhood, children have developed the ability to expand their empathy beyond the domain of family and friends. They begin to care for others who are less advantaged and to show concern for the homeless, the poor, and the chronically ill.

But parents play an important role in keeping the natural feelings of empathy alive in their children by demonstrating tolerance and acceptance of those who are different. Often, a child who bullies does not see empathy modeled at home. Sometimes a child may lack empathy because he or she doesn't feel understood, as if through behavior the child is saying, "Nobody cares what I feel, so why should I care about anybody else?" Not only have these children not learned *how* to be empathic, but they also have not learned the *value* of being empathic. A child can just as easily learn to ignore another person's suffering if he or she is not taught that empathy is highly valued. Parents who tend not to demonstrate empathy need to modify their behavior in order to help their children understand this important value. Observe these two situations to see how parents can model either empathy or intolerance in a passing comment:

Scenario 1

A mother, father, and child wait for a movie to begin. As the coming attractions are running, an obese woman enters and tries to sit. When she finds the seat is too narrow for her, she looks embarrassed, gets up, and leaves the theater. One parent turns to the other and mumbles loudly enough for the child to hear, "Serves her right. If she wants to watch a movie with the rest of us, she can lose some weight. What a fat slob!"

Scenario 2

Another couple waits with their child for the movie to begin. As they witness an obese woman try to sit down and then leave in frustration because the seat was too small, one of the parents remarks, "That's too bad. She must feel embarrassed. They really should have some seats to accommodate larger people."

■ ■ ■

Children are likely to incorporate parental attitudes into their own thinking and behavior. In the first scene, the parents act as if they are superior to the heavyset woman. If a child acquires the attitude that he or she is superior to others, it's more likely that child will display bullying behavior. By making insulting comments about a woman's physical appearance, these parents are teaching their child how to bully. In the second scene, the parents show concern for the same woman. Their child learned a valuable lesson in empathy.

Empathy must be nurtured. Just as a lack of concern for others can be taught, so can a deep respect and love for others. Empathizing with your child is the surest way to help your child learn to empathize with others because he or she has experienced it firsthand. Here are some practical suggestions to help nurture a healthy sense of empathy in your child.

Ask Your Children How They Feel

Feelings are extremely important, and the first step toward helping children learn empathy is to let them know you care about what they feel. Demonstrate empathy by getting in the habit of asking, "How do you feel about that?"

Feelings are often confused with thoughts. Thoughts can be disputed, feelings cannot. Feelings are not interpretations or explanations. You may disagree with your child about whether algebra is a worthwhile subject or whether the Rams will win the Super Bowl, but if your child says he's happy, sad, angry, or scared, that's the bottom line. Feelings cannot be argued. They are the raw stuff of experience, a person's reality reduced to its most honest denominator. When a child is expressing honest feelings, he or she is telling the truth about who he or she is at that moment. It is important to respect that truth.

Give Your Child Unconditional Love

In *To Love and Be Loved: The Difficult Yoga of Relationships,* psychologist Stephen Levine makes the observation that no one has ever been loved enough. You can't spoil a child with too much love or affection. Children need to know that you love them unconditionally no matter how they may behave. Yet too often, people place conditions on loving their children. Some parents send the message that affection and recognition have to be earned by giving children the silent treatment if they misbehave. Others may use kind words as a tool for manipulation, acting affectionately only when they want their children to do something for them.

We all have the same needs to be treated with sensitivity, kindness, and compassion. We all have hearts that grow only by loving, and we all have hearts that have been wounded to various degrees and in different ways. What an opportunity exists for us when we can remember that no matter where we are, no matter who we're with, we can be instruments of healing. Nowhere is this more important than with our children.

Focus on Similarities between Your Child and Others

Help your child understand how others are similar to them, rather than pointing out differences. We have much more in common with each other than we have differences, yet we are often quick to notice and emphasize what sets us apart. Parents must recognize their own prejudices before they will be open enough to help their children confront theirs. Understand your prejudices, and work hard to change them.

Refuse to Tell or Laugh at Cruel or Demeaning Jokes

Take care to tell only jokes that are not mean-spirited. Many jokes are thinly disguised statements of intolerance toward other races, ethnic backgrounds, religions, the opposite gender, or people of different sexual orientations. Show moral courage by kindly challenging intolerant jokes and explaining why you are doing so. Just say, "I don't really think that's very funny because it's intolerant (or unfair, or mean-spirited)." This can seem like a very risky and difficult thing to do when everyone else is laughing, but when you do—especially if children are present—it sends a very important message. If your child tells a mean-spirited joke, it's important to say that such jokes won't be tolerated, and why.

Sometimes when a joke or comment about a child is obviously embarrassing or hurtful to him, a parent dismisses the child's reaction and becomes defensive, saying it was said "just in fun." A child needs to feel free to tell a parent that something doesn't feel OK. If a child says, "I don't like that, please stop," it's important to heed the request without pushing for a reason why. The child has already said why. He or she doesn't like it. This goes for roughhousing and unwanted tickling, as well. Sometimes children won't say that something you've said or done bothers them, so it's important to pay attention to body language and other cues to make sure that what was said in fun is taken in fun.

Be Consciously Kind

Simple, deliberate acts of kindness can have a profound effect on people's lives. And the people who choose to be consciously kind handle stress better, are happier, and have healthier family relationships. Yet most of us tend to go through our lives on autopilot, sleepwalking through our days and reacting to how people treat us, rather than acting *consciously* and choosing to be kind to others regardless of how they may treat us.

Let your children see you practicing a caring attitude toward strangers, like the clerk at the gas station, other drivers on the road, and community members you don't know well. It's easy to be kind to people who are kind to you, but a true attitude of kindness toward others encompasses everyone, even those who may be rude or thoughtless.

Any moment spent in thoughtlessness, bitterness, or unkindness is a moment wasted. Each day, make it a point to be kinder than you were yesterday, and make it a point especially to be consciously kind to your children.

Show Kindness to Animals

Showing kindness to those who are weaker, slower, or unable to defend themselves is well demonstrated by kindness to animals. Many parents fall prey to the "kick the dog" syndrome, and readily pass it on to their children. They've had a rough day and have held in their stress for eight hours, then they come home and lose their patience with the family pet. Be sure to find healthy ways to deal with stress, and always show your children that animals are to be treated with gentleness and kind words.

Follow the Golden Rule

The most common expression of empathy is the Golden Rule: "Do unto others as you would have them do unto you." No matter how it's demonstrated, the Golden Rule is the best rule to follow for any human relationship. It's practical kindness. Make it a rule in your home.

Teaching Your Child to Be a Peacemaker

Peacemaking means seeking nonviolent ways of resolving conflict. This value doesn't come easily but is well worth the effort. Like never before, this world needs peacemakers, and the family is where peace begins. But if we want harmony in our families, peace must begin with each of us as individuals. In families where adults suggest nonviolent ways to manage conflict, bullying is much less likely to occur.

We live in a competitive, "me-first" society, so it's natural that a lot of families fall into behavior patterns that don't emphasize peacemaking. Sometimes it's so easy to make a battle out of the smallest things just to prove a point. Observe the next two situations that are opportunities for peacemaking:

Scenario 1

Seated at the dinner table, a family is enjoying a discussion of the day's events when the phone rings. The mother answers the phone and discovers it's a telemarketer; she is indignant that her dinner has been interrupted. She shouts obscenities into the mouthpiece, slams down the phone, and rants about telemarketers as she sits back down to dinner.

Scenario 2

The family next door is also having dinner when their phone rings. The mother answers the phone, and it's the same telemarketer. The mother is annoyed because her family time was interrupted, but she waits for the caller to pause then replies politely, "No, thank you. I'm not interested. Please remove me from your list, and have a good evening."

■　■　■

In the first scene, we see a mother venting her frustration inappropriately and disrespectfully, teaching her children by example that this is the proper way to deal with stress. Her children are likely to use the same tactics the next time they feel inconvenienced. In the second example, we see a parent who tactfully handles the same annoying situation, yet she treats the person on the other end of the line with dignity and respect.

Here are some practical ideas to help your child develop peaceful behavior.

Use Respectful, Nonphysical Discipline

One of the surest ways you can help reverse a child's bullying behaviors and teach her to be a peacemaker is to learn nonviolent discipline techniques. Consistently refuse to practice physical punishment. Some parents think that society is "too soft" on children who misbehave and that parents need to exert control through physical discipline. Yet physical punishment merely teaches children to use physical force when they want their way. The use of physical discipline also makes it more likely that a parent may strike out in anger, unintentionally harming the child. The best solution is to discontinue any physical discipline you may be using and learn effective nonphysical techniques.

An effective tool for dealing with your child's misbehavior is to use logical consequences instead of punishment. By associating a consequence, or outcome, logically with a behavior, a child is more likely to learn a valuable lesson about why the behavior was inappropriate. Here are two examples of the concept of logical consequences.

Misbehavior	*Logical consequence*
Leaves bicycle in driveway	Bicycle is taken away for a day
Won't eat dinner	No dessert and no evening snack

I'm always amazed that learning how to parent effectively is given such meager attention in our society. We attend years of schooling to learn how to perform in our work careers, but we just assume we already know what to do in the most important career of all—parenting. Learning how to discipline without violence takes time, and the best way to learn is through a parenting class. Affordable and effective programs are available in most communities through churches, synagogues, community education, and social service agencies.

Use Healing Words

Words have the power to hurt or to heal. Be sure to choose your words carefully, and never call your children names, not even a nickname your child doesn't like, or say things when you are stressed that you would not say when you are calm. If you slip and say something hurtful, apologize as soon as you're aware of your mistake.

Children of all ages need to hear words of respect in abundance, so make a lot of room in your vocabulary for "Thank you," "I appreciate that," "I love you," "I'm sorry," and "I forgive you."

Teaching Your Child to Be Responsible

A responsible person is accountable for his or her choices and for the outcome of those choices. A responsible person doesn't make excuses or try to weasel out of obligations. Children need to learn to take responsibility for their own actions. Most children who bully have difficulty with this vital developmental task. They tend to blame others, to try to escape responsibility, and to lie if they need to get their way. They act as if rules were made for others and not for them. These children need their parents to teach them the value of responsibility. Here are two scenes in which a parent has an opportunity to demonstrate responsibility.

Scenario 1

At the last minute, a father is invited to a party that's being thrown to celebrate a friend's birthday. He is scheduled to work and no one can cover for him. His child hears him on the phone telling his boss he has a fever and won't be able to report to work that evening.

Scenario 2

At the last minute, a father is invited to a party that's being thrown to celebrate a friend's birthday. He has been scheduled to work and no one can cover for him. His child hears him on the phone with his friend, wishing him a happy birthday and explaining that he regrets he can't attend the party.

■ ■ ■

In the first scene, the father disregards his responsibility at work so he can attend a party. On top of that, he lies about why he isn't coming in to work. This sends a clear message to his child that such behavior is acceptable. In the second scene, the father takes appropriate responsibility and teaches a valuable lesson to his child—responsibilities take priority over fun.

Helping children who bully learn to take personal responsibility for both good and bad choices is an important role for parents, and parents can put the following attitudes and behaviors into practice to ensure that a child will learn how to be responsible.

Have a Positive Attitude toward Parenting

Children need to know that their parents fully and gladly accept responsibility for them. What an awesome and joyful responsibility it is to raise a child. Parenting is a role that should be celebrated, not seen as a dreary obligation.

Some parents of children who bully tell their children in subtle or blatant ways that they are unwanted, a nuisance, or a burden. If you have viewed parenting as a chore, it's important that you work to change this attitude and learn to appreciate your important role. Kids' needs can't be a burden. Your child is counting on you.

Let your child know you cherish being his parent. The most important way for your child to learn responsibility is for him to know that you take your responsibility as a parent seriously, and that you'll never give up on your child.

Be a Model of Honesty at All Times

Being a responsible person means being honest. Honesty is essential to a child's ability to form lasting relationships. Children who bully often don't know that trustworthiness is a highly prized virtue. They don't understand that dishonesty breeds distrust and erodes relationships like nothing else, so they jeopardize connections with peers, parents, teachers, and adults in the neighborhood.

Parents are in a vital position to instill the importance of honesty through role modeling. If a parent is trustworthy in all things, it is likely that a child will follow that example. Being honest entails taking responsibility for our own actions. Don't expect your child to keep a standard that you won't keep. Trustworthiness must be demonstrated and expected by being radically honest in your dealings with your children, as well as your dealings with anyone else. Being trustworthy does not mean getting away with what you can. When a child hears "Don't let me see you doing that again," it teaches the child to try to avoid getting caught. She should know there's no room for dishonesty in any situation, no matter how easy it may be to fabricate an excuse to her advantage.

Provide Good Supervision

Helping children learn to be responsible means letting children know that you will be there for them until they can adequately take care of themselves. Children who bully need parents to spend quality time with them. They often feel as if their parents don't care about their thoughts or feelings. These children need to know that they're understood and that their successes, their disappointments, and their dreams are important to their parents.

Talk with your kids. Get to know them as people. Have fun with them, and really listen to them without preaching at them. Spend time with each of your children every day, even if it's only a few minutes. Let them know how very important they are to you, and that you'll be there for them when they have a problem.

As a general rule, children under ten should never be left home alone, but you may want to check your state's laws to see what age applies in your community. If you will be gone for even a short time, arrange for someone you trust to watch young children. Children ten or older may be responsible for themselves up to an hour or more, depending upon the child's maturity. When children are left at home, be sure a support system is available in case they need help. Be sure your children know emergency phone numbers, and how to get in contact with you immediately. If a child is to be responsible for the care of younger children, be sure that the child is mature enough and has the skills to handle the job. To prepare your child for that responsibility, consider having him take the American Red Cross baby-sitter's training program, a one-day class that teaches children ages eleven to fifteen important skills, such as first aid, lifesaving techniques, and decision making.

Know where your children are at all times and who their friends are. This becomes especially important for parents of children who bully, because these children may associate with other aggressive children. Don't allow your child to have friends of whom you don't approve at your home while you're gone. If work requires you to be away from home in the summer or during after-school hours, encourage your children to participate in supervised after-school activities such as sports, drama, tutoring, or youth programs.

Be Cooperative and Supportive with the School and with Your Child's Other Parent(s)

Some parents get caught up in power struggles with the other parent, with the child's stepparents, or with school authorities. It is important that your child sees you doing your best to cooperate with other adults who are responsible for your child's welfare. Respect the opinions of other adults who are important in your child's life, even though you may not agree. If you cannot speak with the child's other parent or stepparents without arguing, you may want to consider individual or family therapy, or mediation from a trained mediator, to improve communication. Let the school know that you are working to help change your child's behavior, and offer to cooperate in any way you can to help your child resolve problems at school. If you are proactive rather than reactive with other adults involved in your child's life, you will find that you gain much more support, and solution finding becomes a team effort.

Admit Your Mistakes

Part of learning responsibility means admitting when you're wrong. This isn't easy and takes courage. Through modeling, parents need to show their children how to own up to their mistakes. So admit when you're wrong and make necessary amends to correct the problem.

Cooperatively Decide Upon Age-Appropriate Chores

Children learn responsibility by having opportunities to practice it. Children should have regular household chores that fit their skills and ages. They shouldn't expect any reward other than knowing they are important contributors to the daily functioning of their family. Though allowances are useful to help children learn to manage money, allowances should never be attached to household chores. This leads children to be willing to help only if they will see a monetary reward for their work, which is not the way the world works. Children will soon learn the satisfaction of completing a task and helping the family and will not mind the lack of monetary compensation for their work.

Be sure to explain clearly and demonstrate what, when, and how the tasks are to be done. School-age children can handle two or three small daily jobs and a larger weekly job. Following are some suggestions for household chores:

- For ages six to nine: Keep own bedroom clean and tidy, make bed, empty wastebaskets, sweep floors, help prepare meals, set table, help wash dishes, pull weeds, water plants, and answer telephone and take messages.

- For ages ten and up: All of the above, plus wash the family car, dust furniture, help with laundry, mow lawn (may need supervision), clean bathroom, and give pets food and water.

It is helpful to have children choose the chores for which they will be responsible, because when a child has a stake in the decision-making process, she's more likely to get the task done without being reminded. You can hold a family meeting at which time you provide a list of possible options. If there is more than one child in the family, chores can be rotated according to what is decided in the family meeting. Family meetings are a very helpful way to improve family harmony and communication; more information can be found in *The Parent's Handbook: Systematic Training for Effective Parenting*, by Don Dinkmeyer and Garry McKay.

When to Seek Professional Help

When a child's serious behavior problems continue despite your best efforts, professional help is necessary. Seeing a psychologist, social worker, or psychiatrist is highly recommended if your child

- Enjoys intimidating, threatening, or harming others
- Has used objects or weapons to harm or threaten other people
- Often starts fights with peers
- Has threatened or harmed another child sexually
- Destroys other people's property
- Lies repeatedly
- Usually blames others for own misbehavior
- Consistently does not listen to adults

- Often breaks parental curfew or is truant from school
- Is cruel to animals

Knowing how to treat others with respect is essential if your child is to develop the values of empathy, peacemaking, and responsibility. Dealing with anger is a difficult challenge for any of us, and particularly so with children who bully. The focus of the next chapter is helping your child learn to handle anger respectfully.

11

Helping Your Child Deal with Anger

Children who bully have difficulty with excessive and inappropriately expressed anger. They often respond to the slightest and most innocent provocation, like getting bumped in the hallway or on the playground, with unwarranted angry words and actions. These children need help with learning how to deal with anger in socially responsible ways. The best way for parents to teach a child who bullies how to handle anger is by modeling effective anger management at home and teaching the child how to communicate his needs so that others are likely to listen. To help our children with anger, we need to begin by examining how we as parents understand and handle anger ourselves.

What Are Your Beliefs about Anger?

Ask yourself what happened the last time you got angry. What hurt you? Who hurt you? How did the pain feel? Were you intimidated? Discounted? Ignored? Made to appear stupid? Physically hurt? Whatever happened, your anger was a response to pain of some kind, either emotional or physical pain. Life is often painful, and no one can escape that reality. When we are in pain, we don't want to be vulnerable and expose ourselves to further pain, so we send a message to those around us that says, "Don't hurt me anymore!" That's anger.

There's nothing wrong with anger. In itself, anger is not dangerous or bad. In fact, anger can be a very beneficial emotion because it helps alert us to what is painful and mobilizes us to protect ourselves from further hurt. But anger is such a physical feeling—hearts pump, adrenaline rushes, skin flushes, bodies tense—that it can also be a difficult emotion to handle.

Many children are afraid of anger because they associate it with abuse they have experienced when someone else was angry. When children are hit, screamed at, or called names by other children or by adults, they may think that anger itself is dangerous, when in fact it's the abusive behavior that's dangerous. Children who see the adults around them mishandle anger often respond to it inappropriately themselves. It's this mismanagement of anger that can lead children to harm others or themselves.

But there is no need for anger to lead to physical or emotional damage, because anger is controllable. People say, "It just comes over me" or "I can't help it when I lose my temper—I never have any warning." But there really are warning signs that herald an angry episode. People with anger problems have learned not to pay attention to feelings that precede an explosive outburst. They usually have a hard time recognizing more subtle feelings like irritation or annoyance and can only recognize powerful feelings like extreme anger. People sometimes say they don't have the willpower to control their anger, but it's not so much a matter of willpower as "skill power." Learning to handle and express anger respectfully and appropriately is a skill like any other skill, one that is acquired by hard work, determination, and practice. Think of anger as being not just one feeling but a range of feelings, starting with milder feelings of annoyance and leading up to more intense feelings of anger and finally rage. Learning to pay attention to the feelings that precede or accompany anger allows us to recognize it while it is still manageable.

Some people mistakenly believe and mistakenly teach their children that responses to anger are completely inherent. How you express anger is not genetic, nor is it determined by gender, race, or socioeconomic class. We often hear that someone has a short fuse, as if a fusebox actually exists somewhere! Or "What can you expect—she's German (or Irish, or Italian, or from the other side of the tracks)." When people say they can't help what they're like when they get angry, they willingly surrender their ability to choose how they will respond to anger.

We often hear people incorrectly say, "You make me so mad." No one has the ability to make you angry. Anger is always a choice. What we mean when we say someone *makes* us angry is that we've been hurt. Sometimes we think that gives us the right to hurt him or her back. But instead of stooping to an angry tirade, we can choose to express our pain clearly and calmly. When we're hurt, we can say, "That hurts! I want you to stop!" And we can teach our children to be just as calm and respectful when they get angry.

When Is a Parent's Anger Excessive?

Your primary role as parent is to teach your child how to be responsible and loving. It's natural to feel angry sometimes when children misbehave, don't listen, talk back, or violate family rules, but it's at those times that you must have control of your anger and be responsible and loving toward your child. If you are too angry to be kind, you are too angry to discipline your child at that moment.

Anger is excessive and inappropriately expressed when a parent

- Swears at a child
- Strikes a child
- Throws an object at a child
- Threatens to physically harm a child
- Calls the child names or insults the child by poking at a child's weak points
- Tries to scare a child
- Yells or screams at a child

If you feel like doing any of these, remove yourself from the situation and take a time-out immediately!

How Excessive Parental Anger Affects Children

Excessive anger is a particular problem in families of children who bully. All parents get angry with their children from time to time, and many parents feel guilty about the levels of anger they feel and express toward their children. Some parents don't feel bad about showing excessive anger because they don't think it's harmful. But excessive and inappropriately expressed anger is very harmful to children. In addition, the results that angry behavior produces are usually the opposite of those the parent wants. Kids who have a parent who expresses anger inappropriately tend to be less respectful of the parent and the parent's authority, leading to even more disobedience. Here are common problems that occur when anger is excessive.

Children May Become Less Cooperative

Parents try to demand greater cooperation by losing their temper, but paradoxically this usually just leads to more defiance. When parents get excessively angry, children are less likely to cooperate. Who wants to cooperate with someone who is yelling at them? It's unrealistic to believe that a child will be induced toward greater cooperation when she is being treated disrespectfully.

Children May Become Angry and Seek Revenge Inappropriately

Parental shouting, name-calling, or physical discipline leave a child feeling angry with the parent. Since some children who bully don't feel safe expressing their anger with their parents, they take it out on peers at school who are unlikely to fight back.

Children May Become Fearful

A parent's excessive anger leaves some children afraid, even terrified, of a parent. Children who bully are often so out of touch with their feelings that they are not aware they are afraid and present only an angry facade to the world. Expressing fear requires that a child feel safe that he won't be ridiculed for it, and children who fear their parents don't feel safe. Until theorists such as Rudolf Dreikurs, who wrote *Children: The Challenge*, began changing our cultural awareness of effective parenting in the 1960s, tradition in our society relied heavily upon the use of fear and abuse to dominate children. Unfortunately, even some contemporary parenting books advise parents that it's beneficial for their children to fear them. But most people consider this attitude outmoded and support thinking that says love can never grow where fear has taken root.

Children May Feel Shamed

Children subjected to excessive parental anger are likely to feel shamed. Shame leaves the child feeling as if there is something inherently wrong with who she *is*, not with what the child has done. When a parent overreacts with anger, putting down a child with humiliating words, for example, the child may feel attacked as a person. Children who bully are often the targets of expressions of parental anger that lead to shame. Although these children are not bad people, their parents' anger leads them to think of themselves as bad. They torment other children to convince themselves that others are even more unlovable than they are. To prevent your child from developing a sense of shame, it's important to remember to separate the child from any misbehavior. Though the misbehavior isn't valued, your child should always be valued.

How to Change the Way You Handle Anger

If you were unaware of how your anger affects your child and now have begun to feel that you've done irreversible harm, don't worry that all is lost. You can still help a child who bullies learn to control his anger. Modeling effective anger management yourself is the best way to teach this to your child. When your child sees you dealing with anger in a positive way, he will likely follow your lead. Through careful modeling, your child learns that anger is a normal emotion, not an excuse to control someone else. It will likely be hard for you to change your old behaviors and put new ones into practice, as you probably learned much about how to handle anger as a very young child and your responses seem automatic, but you can do it. If you slip and behave inappropriately, apologize and try again. Here are some valuable suggestions for you to practice at home.

Know When You're Angry

Tom came home after an especially stressful day at work to find that his ten-year-old son had left his bicycle in the driveway again. He felt flushed, his heart was racing, and he noticed he was taking short, quick breaths. These physical sensations were Tom's signals that he was getting very angry and needed to calm down before he dealt with the problem of his son's bicycle.

It's important to pay attention to the physiological cues that tell us we're getting angry. Anger is a powerful emotional state that produces unmistakable physiological reactions, such as the following:

- Elevated body temperature
- Increased heart rate
- Dizziness
- Shortness of breath
- Rapid breathing
- Sweating
- Tightness in the arms, chest, hands, and stomach
- Nervous stomach ("butterflies")
- Jaw clenching or grinding

When you notice any of these signals, take the time to calm down before doing anything else. When parents discipline in anger, they are more likely to be unfair and impulsive and to harm their children physically or emotionally.

Take a Time-Out

When Tom saw his son's bike in the driveway, then noticed how he felt and identified the feeling as anger, he said to himself, "Stop and think. I can handle this calmly." He sat in his car for a minute, took some deep breaths, and waited until he felt calm before he went in to talk with his son. This was Tom's way of taking a time-out.

The old idea of taking a time-out is one of the best and most effective ways to deal with anger. Whatever is causing the anger needs to be dealt with, but until you get a little distance and calm down, you won't be rational.

Teach your children the value of cooling off with a time-out, using three steps:

1. **Stop.** Stop doing what you're doing. Whatever the problem is, it can wait until you cool down. Keeping your composure is the most important goal right now.

2. **Think.** Talk to yourself using positive self-statements like "No yelling," "This too shall pass," "I can think this through calmly," "I am peaceful and calm," "I treat my child with love and respect," or "Stop! Think!" It's hard to think straight when you're angry, so choose one positive self-statement in advance, or combine a couple as Tom did, to say to yourself whenever you're angry.

3. **Breathe.** Taking a breather is one of the quickest and most effective ways to calm down from anger. Focus *all* of your attention on your breathing. Inhale through your nose and exhale through your mouth. Taking easy, slow breaths, say to yourself, "Breathe in . . . relax." Imagine that you're inhaling peace and calmness and exhaling anger. Allow yourself to breathe like this until you are calm.

If you continue to feel too angry to talk kindly, you need to remove yourself from the situation. Just tell your child, "I'm too angry right now to talk, and I'm going to take a time-out." Then get away from the situation for a little while until you are able to talk calmly. You may want to take a walk, write out your feelings in a letter, or do some physical work to discharge your energy. Don't drink alcohol or take any other drugs or drive a car while you're taking your time-out.

It's most important to remember to be loving with your child at all times—especially when you're angry, and taking a time-out enables that to happen.

Use Positive Coping Thoughts

Parents who handle frustration well tend to use positive self-talk. Practice paying attention to the thoughts that race through your mind when you are angry. Often, they are negative thoughts that only intensify the anger. When you catch this happening, challenge these negative thoughts with more realistic, positive thoughts. For example:

Instead of saying to your child	*Say to yourself*
"I can't stand this."	"I can handle this. It's a challenge, but I can handle it."
"You're trying to drive me crazy."	"This is normal for her age. My child is not trying to drive me crazy. She is just being a normal kid."
"You never listen."	"That's not true. Sometimes he does. Right now, he's upset and has his own agenda. I'm the adult, and I can behave like one. I will treat him with respect."
"You are (a jerk, a bum, lazy, stupid, etc.)."	"Take it easy. Name-calling won't help anything. Just because I'm angry doesn't give me the right to disrespect her. I will use respectful language even though I'm angry."
"You always turn things into an argument."	"Don't exaggerate. Sometimes he doesn't. I can be calm and adult about this."
"You don't care about me."	"Hold it. I don't know what she feels. She is acting self-centered right now, but so what? That's how children act sometimes when they're not getting their needs met. I will be calm and treat her with respect."

Helpful Ideas for Children
to Deal with Anger

Families often have unspoken rules about anger. In some families, expressing anger in any way is not allowed. Other families are just the opposite. In these families, anger seems to be the only feeling that's ever expressed. Neither polarity is healthy. Let anger be acceptable in your family, but always insist that it's expressed respectfully.

Never deny a child's anger by saying things like, "I know you're not really angry" or "I know you don't really feel that way." This isn't only insulting to a child, it drives the anger underground. Unexpressed feelings always find an outlet, and so will anger, whether in acting out violently or in depression.

A parent who denies a child's anger is uncomfortable with his or her own feelings. If you have a hard time accepting or feeling anger yourself, it is likely that your children will, too. Families need ground rules for expressing anger. Modeling appropriate anger management is a big portion of correcting your child's inappropriate behavior, but children who bully also need some direct guidance on the attitudes and skills necessary for effective anger management. The suggestions that follow will help your children control their anger physically and verbally.

Teach Your Child Never to Hit, Throw Things at Others, or Call Names

Anger is a physical feeling, and some children like to hit people or throw things at them when they're angry. Teach your children never to touch anyone when they are angry and never to pick up anything to throw at people. Teach your children never to use names or words that *could possibly* hurt another's feelings.

Teach Your Child the Difference between Fear and Respect

Children who bully often confuse fear with respect. They think that people won't respect them if they stop bullying. Your child needs to learn that fear and respect are mutually incompatible. Children who bully are often surprised to discover that people actually show them more respect when they start treating people fairly. When they discover that they can often get what they want by treating someone with respect, they will stop depending on the tool they've used so long—intimidation.

The best way to teach your child how to treat people with respect is to encourage your child to respect you, not fear you. Respect is built by ensuring that you always treat your child with dignity and kindness. Don't discipline when you are angry. Children whose parents respect them will naturally respect their parents in turn and will seek the advice and guidance of parents in times of trouble.

Think of the Consequences

When a child feels angry, it's time for him to think. There is always a choice in how to express anger. Help your child see that at the point of anger, what he decides to do is a choice—nothing *pushes* one into negative behavior. Teach your child that no one *makes* you angry, but that to react with anger is a decision he makes. Teach your child to stop and ask himself, "What will the consequences be if I lose my temper, and what will they be if I keep my temper?" And then, "Which consequences do I want?" Negative consequences may mean losing privileges at school, losing privileges at home, or getting hurt. A positive consequence for controlling anger, besides retaining privileges, may be earning the respect of other children.

Anger, a necessary emotion for our survival, helps protect us from unnecessary harm. When handled poorly and used as an excuse to harm others either physically or verbally, it leads to conflict. When handled well, the expression of anger helps us resolve conflict. Parents are in a prime position to teach a child who bullies how to express anger respectfully and safely.

Epilogue for All Parents

Broad societal changes take time and continuous effort. Two hundred years ago, law-abiding U.S. citizens legally owned other human beings. Until the early part of the last century, women were legally considered inferior to men in the United States. Less than fifty years ago, it was legal to bar people from using a public facility because of their skin color. We look back now and wonder how our nation could have accepted such inhumane notions. Although we still have a great distance to go to ensure the civil rights of all people, the law now provides for racial and gender equality.

However, if we are to reach a point where we can consider racism and sexism and other attitudes of intolerance to be problems of the past, we must confront our attitudes about childhood peer abuse. After all, if we're serious about changing the violent social texture of this nation and reducing our prison populations, we must start with our children. The seeds of adult intolerance and criminal behavior are sown in childhood. We must recognize that when we minimize bullying in childhood, we normalize violent behavior. When we normalize child-to-child violence, we can expect to continue reaping a terrible harvest. Without effective intervention, children who bully will go on to drag down our society with violence as adults. And targets of peer abuse can become violent themselves, especially when they feel no one cares.

Just punishing children with antisocial tendencies does not and will not work. But we have often failed to look beyond punishment of children who bully as a solution to peer abuse. Though punishment is often appropriate and necessary, punishment alone does not go far enough toward teaching children to be accountable for their behavior. To stop peer abuse, we must help children who bully learn the values, attitudes, and behaviors—especially empathy and anger management—

that are conducive to healthy peer relationships. Part of learning accountability must come from the family. A family is a learning laboratory for a child. Children learn wonderful things in families. But from family, children can also learn behavior that's disrespectful to others and ultimately self-defeating. If a child isn't learning accountability for his behavior at home, both the child and the family need help.

Families of children who are targets of peer abuse also have a role to play in changing the damaging effects of peer abuse in our society. They can help a child develop healthy self-esteem and assertiveness skills, which prepare the child to effectively cope with the behavior of aggressive children. If enough children are taught to refuse to accept the attitudes of superiority and entitlement that aggressive children display, children who bully will learn that this behavior won't be tolerated and won't pay off even in the short run.

Beyond the family, we also need more comprehensive programs to help young people. Fighting the battle against peer abuse requires a concerted effort on the part of parents, schools, the legal system, and the community at large. As parents, we need to band together with schools and communities to stop peer abuse. Our children deserve to live their lives free from the fear of abuse of any type, and our efforts to help our children develop healthier patterns of behavior can change the course of their lives.

Notes

Introduction

1. J. Hoover, R. Oliver, and K. Thomson, "Perceived Victimization by School Bullies: New Research and Future Direction," *Journal of Humanistic Education and Development* 32 (1993): 76–84.

2. R. Hazler, J. Hoover, and R. Oliver, "What Kids Say about Bullying," *Executive Educator* 14, no. 11 (1992): 20–22.

3. J. Lee, *Facing the Fire: Experiencing and Expressing Anger Appropriately* (New York: Bantam Books, 1993).

Chapter 1

1. Lesa Rae Vartanian, personal communication, Indiana University–Purdue University, Fort Wayne, Ind., November 1999.

Chapter 2

1. M. A. Hamburg, "Youth Violence Is a Public Health Concern," *Violence in American Schools: A New Perspective,* ed. D. S. Elliott, B. Hamburg, and K. R. Williams (New York: Cambridge University Press, 1998), 31–54.

2. Database online: http://www.cdc.gov/ncipc/osp/usmort.htm, Atlanta, Ga.: Centers for Disease Control and Prevention, National Center for Injury Prevention and Control. Accessed August 1999.

3. Centers for Disease Control and Prevention, "Rates of Homicide, Suicide, and Firearm-Related Deaths among Children in Twenty-Six Industrialized Countries," *Morbidity and Mortality Weekly Report* 46 (1997): 101–5.

4. Gesele Lajoie, Alyson McLellan, and Cindi Seddon, *Take Action against Bullying* (Coquitlam, B.C.: Bully B'Ware Productions, 1997).

5. G. M. Batsche and H. M. Knoff, "Bullies and Their Victims: Understanding a Pervasive Problem in the Schools," *School Psychology Review* 23, no. 2 (1994): 165–74.

6. R. Oliver, J. Hoover, and R. Hazler, "The Perceived Roles of Bullying in Small-Town Midwestern Schools," *Journal of Counseling and Development* 72 (1994): 416–20.

7. H. Estroff Marano, "Big, Bad Bully," *Psychology Today,* September/October 1995, 50–82.

8. Betty Reardon, keynote address, "Peacebuilding in Schools and Communities," Indiana University, Bloomington, Ind., August 15, 1999.

Chapter 3

1. D. Olweus, "Bully/Victim Problems among Schoolchildren: Basic Facts and Effects of a School-Based Intervention Program," *The Development and Treatment of Childhood Aggression* (Hillsdale, N.J.: Lawrence Erlbaum, 1991), 411–48.

2. Judith Rich Harris, *The Nurture Assumption* (New York: The Free Press, 1998).

3. P. T. Slee, "Situational and Interpersonal Correlates of Anxiety Associated with Peer Victimization," *Child Psychiatry and Human Development* 25, no. 2 (1994): 97–107.

4. G. M. Batsche and H. M. Knoff, "Bullies and Their Victims: Understanding a Pervasive Problem in the Schools," *School Psychology Review* 23, no. 2 (1994): 165–74.

5. S. Greenbaum, B. Turner, and R. D. Stephens, *Set Straight on Bullies* (Los Angeles: Pepperdine University Press, 1988).

6. D. Olweus, "Schoolyard Bullying: Grounds for Intervention," *School Safety,* Fall 1987, 4–11; L. D. Eron, "Aggression through the Ages," *School Safety,* Fall 1987, 12–16.

7. V. E. Besag, *Bullies and Victims in Schools* (Bristol, Pa.: Open University Press, 1989).

8. D. Olweus, "Victimization by Peers: Antecedents and Long-term Outcomes," *Social Withdrawal, Inhibitions, and Shyness,* ed. K. H. Rubin and J. B. Asendorf (Hillsdale, N.J.: Lawrence Erlbaum, 1993), 315–41.

9. L. Eron, "What Becomes of Aggressive School-children?" *Harvard Mental Health Letter,* April 1988, 8.

Chapter 9

1. D. Gorman-Smith, P. H. Tolan, A. Zelli, and L. R. Huesmann, "The Relation of Family Functioning to Violence among Inner-City Minority Youths," *Journal of Family Psychology* 10 (1996): 115–29.

Recommended Reading

Dinkmeyer, Don, and Gary McKay. *The Parent's Handbook: Systematic Training for Effective Parenting.* Circle Pines, Minn.: American Guidance Service, 1997.

Eastman, Meg, and Sydney Craft Rosen. *Taming the Dragon in Your Child: Solutions for Breaking the Cycle of Family Anger.* New York: Wiley, 1994.

Hyman, Irwin A. *The Case against Spanking: How to Discipline Your Child without Hitting.* San Francisco, Calif.: Jossey-Bass, 1997.

Illsley Clarke, Jeanne, and Connie Dawson. *Growing Up Again: Parenting Ourselves, Parenting Our Children.* 2d ed. Center City, Minn.: Hazelden Information and Educational Services, 1998.

Lighter, Don. *Gentle Discipline: Fifty Effective Techniques for Teaching Your Children Good Behavior.* Minnetonka, Minn.: Meadowbrook Press, 1995.

McKay, Matthew, Patrick Fanning, Kim Paleg, and Dana Landis. *When Anger Hurts Your Kids: A Parent's Guide.* Oakland, Calif.: New Harbinger, 1996.

Nelson, Jane, Lynn Lott, and H. Stephen Glenn. *Positive Discipline A–Z.* Rocklin, Calif.: Prima, 1999.

Index

About the Author

William Voors, a licensed clinical social worker, has counseled individuals and families for more than twenty years. In addition to his psychotherapy practice, Mr. Voors conducts bullying awareness and prevention workshops for schools and community agencies. He and his wife live in Fort Wayne, Indiana, and are the parents of two grown sons.

About the Publisher

Hazelden Information and Educational Services is a division of the Hazelden Foundation, a not-for-profit organization. Since 1949, Hazelden has been a leader in promoting the dignity and treatment of people afflicted with the disease of chemical dependency.

The mission of the foundation is to improve the quality of life for individuals, families, and communities by providing a national continuum of information, education, and recovery services that are widely accessible; to advance the field through research and training; and to improve our quality and effectiveness through continuous improvement and innovation.

Stemming from that, the mission of this division is to provide quality information and support to people wherever they may be in their personal journey—from education and early intervention, through treatment and recovery, to personal and spiritual growth.

Although our treatment programs do not necessarily use everything Hazelden publishes, our bibliotherapeutic materials support our mission and the Twelve Step philosophy upon which it is based. We encourage your comments and feedback.

The headquarters of the Hazelden Foundation are in Center City, Minnesota. Additional treatment facilities are located in Chicago, Illinois; New York, New York; Plymouth, Minnesota; St. Paul, Minnesota; and West Palm Beach, Florida. At these sites, we provide a continuum of care for men and women of all ages. Our Plymouth facility is designed specifically for youth and families.

For more information on Hazelden, please call **1-800-257-7800.** Or you may access our World Wide Web site on the Internet at **http://www.hazelden.org.**